T0321622

Opinion Analysis
for Online Reviews

East China Normal University Scientific Reports
Subseries on Data Science and Engineering

ISSN: 2382-5715

Chief Editor
Weian Zheng
Changjiang Chair Professor
School of Finance and Statistics
East China Normal University, China
Email: financialmaths@gmail.com

Associate Chief Editor
Shanping Wang
Senior Editor
Journal of East China Normal University (Natural Sciences), China
Email: spwang@library.ecnu.edu.cn

East China Normal University Scientific Reports | Vol. 4
Subseries on Data Science and Engineering

Opinion Analysis for Online Reviews

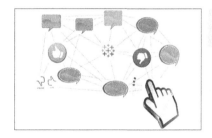

Yuming Lin
Guilin University of Electronic Technology, China

Xiaoling Wang
East China Normal University, China

Aoying Zhou
East China Normal University, China

 **World Scientific**

NEW JERSEY · LONDON · SINGAPORE · BEIJING · SHANGHAI · HONG KONG · TAIPEI · CHENNAI · TOKYO

Published by

World Scientific Publishing Co. Pte. Ltd.

5 Toh Tuck Link, Singapore 596224

USA office: 27 Warren Street, Suite 401-402, Hackensack, NJ 07601

UK office: 57 Shelton Street, Covent Garden, London WC2H 9HE

Library of Congress Cataloging-in-Publication Data

Names: Lin, Yuming, 1978– author. | Wang, Xiaoling, 1975– author. |
 Zhou, Aoying, 1965– author.

Title: Opinion analysis for online reviews / Yuming Lin (Guilin University of
 Electronic Technology, China), Xiaoling Wang (East China Normal University, China) &
 Aoying Zhou (East China Normal University, China).

Description: New Jersey : World Scientific, [2016] | Series: East China Normal University
 Scientific Reports ; volume 4 | Includes bibliographical references.

Identifiers: LCCN 2016000703| ISBN 9789813100435 (hc : alk. paper) |
 ISBN 9789813100442 (pbk : alk. paper)

Subjects: LCSH: Public opinion. | Internet users--Attitudes. | Consumers--Attitudes. |
 Data mining. | Web sites--Public opinion. | Web sites--Ratings and rankings.

Classification: LCC HM1236 .L56 2016 | DDC 025.042--dc23

LC record available at https://lccn.loc.gov/2016000703

British Library Cataloguing-in-Publication Data

A catalogue record for this book is available from the British Library.

Desk Editor: Herbert Moses

Typeset by Stallion Press
Email: enquiries@stallionpress.com

Printed in Singapore

East China Normal University Scientific Reports

Preface

With the development of Web2.0, more and more users prefer to share their opinions with online reviews, which are opinion-rich and play important roles in many Web applications like business and government intelligence, analysis of public opinions on Internet, question answering system and personalized recommendation system. Such Web applications depend on the correct identification of user opinions. Then, automatic detection of user opinions expressed in massive reviews becomes an urgent demand, and has seen a great deal of attention in recent years.

Compared with traditional text analysis tasks, opinion analysis is more difficult due to the flexibility and complexity of opinion expression. The informal review contents with huge data volume bring more new challenges. On the other hand, opinion analysis contains more research contents, it includes the quality control of opinion texts, opinion information extraction, opinion identification, opinion summarization and retrieval, which is penetrating from data collection and integration to providing analytical results for the users and Web services in next stage. The quality control of opinion texts provides reliable data for the subsequent applications and researches, whereas the opinion identification provides the important information for opinion summarization and retrieval in the opinion analysis process. Then, we focus on these tow topics in this book, and our contributions are as follows.

(1) Proposing a new feature function via integrating the term's sentiment information with its contribution to a document, which is an important part of feature presentation. By the proposed method, the poor effectiveness of sentiment classification with traditional feature functions used in text classification is improved, which do not consider the term's sentiment information. At first, we capture the term's sentiment orientation by evaluating the term's mutual information with the sentiment labels. Secondly, we determine the feature's

value via integrating the term's sentiment score and its contribution to a document. The experimental results show that the proposed method is more effective than those traditional ones in sentiment classification.

(2) Proposing a three phase framework for sentiment classification, by which a set of sentiment classifiers are selected to make predictions, and these predictions are integrated via ensemble learning. We propose a quality evaluation criterion for a set of classifiers based on classifier's accuracies and diversity, which can determine a set of optimal classifier used for assemble. We devise a *stacking*-based ensemble learning algorithm to integrate multiple predictions generated by the selected classifiers. The proposed method overcomes the best traditional single classifier method in different domains.

(3) Proposing a greedy algorithm for classifier set selection, which solve the problem of combination explosion encountered during the process of classifier set selection. At first, we transform the classifier set selection into an optimization problem. Then, we devise a greedy algorithm for selecting a set of classifiers based on the candidate's accuracies and diversity. We prove the greedy algorithm to be 2-approximation, which guarantees the quality of selected classifiers. Moreover, the proposed algorithm's time complexity is $O(N)$ (N is the number of optional classifiers), which enhances the availability of the three phase ensemble learning framework for sentiment classification greatly.

(4) Proposing six features for review spam detection based on modeling the review contents and reviewer's behaviors, and devising a supervised review spam detection algorithm and a threshold-based one respectively. The proposed algorithms can identify the review spam in time, which cannot be done by the existing methods. Furthermore, high identification precision, and recall on review spam can be achieved by the proposed algorithms. Especially, the threshold-based algorithm can obtain good effectiveness without labeled samples.

In summary, we focus on four problems including the feature presentation for opinion analysis, multiple classifiers ensemble learning for opinion analysis, the strategy of classifier set selection, and the online review spam detection. These research contents have coherence and sustainability, and form a relatively complete research.

Yuming Lin
Xiaoling Wang
Aoying Zhou

Acknowledgments

This work was supported by National Science Foundation of China (No. 61562014, 61363005, 61170085 and 61472141), 973 project (2010CB328106), NSFC-Guangdong United Foundation Project (No. U1501252), Guangxi Natural Science Foundation (No. 2013GXNSFBA019267, 2015GXNSFAA139303), the project of Guangxi Key Laboratory of Trusted Software, the high level of innovation team of Colleges and Universities in Guangxi and outstanding scholars program funding.

We can't thank all the people who have made contributions and suggestions to this book, but we would like to acknowledge especially the help of Kun Yue, Jingwei Zhang, Zhao Zhang, Tao Zhu, Chen Xu, Keqiang Wang, and Bing Zhao. We would like to express our sincere thanks and appreciation to the people at the University Press, for their generous help throughout the publication preparation process.

Acknowledgments

Contents

Chapter 1

Introduction

With the development and popularization of Web2.0, the communication forms of network users have changed dramatically. More and more users prefer to browse, post and repost messages on various social network platforms to share opinions and experience with others. At the same time, the development of social network techniques and the transformation of user communication have had a great influence on e-commerce area. An open network environment would provide a broad space and convenient way for many practical applications, such as e-commerce/e-government and advertising serving.

On the other hand, the rich opinions in online reviews serve as a valuable reference for government departments, manufacturers, merchants and customers. By reading the reviews, the consumers can know about the features of products, providers can know about what the consumers care about on their products. According to the survey[1] released by Cone in 2011, before deciding whether to purchase recommended products or services, 81% consumers will go online to verify those recommendations, specifically through researching product/service information (61%), reading user reviews (55%) or searching rating websites (43%). About four-out-of-five consumers have changed their purchase intention based solely on negative information. And positive information has a similar influence on decision making. As a result, online reviews are very important to a product/service on the Web, it brings an urgent demand on identifying the users' opinions expressed in reviews automatically.

1.1 The research framework on opinion analysis

Opinion analysis, also called opinion mining, sentiment analysis [Pang and Lee (2008)], involves the processes of analysis, processing, induction and deduction

[1] Available at http://www.conecomm.com/2011coneonlineinfluencetrendtracker

1

for text. In this book, we use these terms more or less interchangeably. The study on opinion analysis has received increasing attention by industry insiders and academics, which involves many challenging tasks like review quality evaluation, opinion information extraction, opinion identification, opinion retrieval and opinion summarization. Figure 1.1 shows the research framework on opinion analysis.

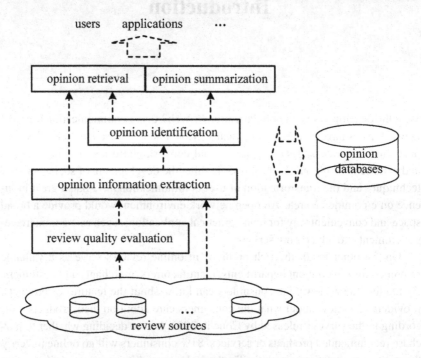

Fig. 1.1   The research framework on opinion analysis

As one of the main ways on sentiment expression, the text from various sources is quite different on quality. For example, the reviews from authoritative sites would have high quality, those from the public review sites would encounter the quality problem, even the malicious reviews deviating from the facts. Such reviews are called review spam [Jindal and Liu (2008)], which should be filtered out before analyzing the opinion expressed in reviews. The techniques on review spam detection target at identifying the review spam [Jindal and Liu (2008); Li *et al.* (2011); Ott *et al.* (2011); Xie *et al.* (2012); Jindal *et al.* (2010)], the review spammers [Lee *et al.* (2010); Lim *et al.* (2010)], and the suspicious reviewer groups [Mukherjee *et al.* (2011, 2012)]. In order to reduce the negative impacts made by review spam, they should be detected as early as possible. The review quality can be evaluated by review's readability, product feature coverage, product relevance, reviewer's expertise and so on [Kim and Movy (2006); Lu *et al.* (2010); Liu *et al.* (2008); P O'Mahony and Smyth (2009)]. It is worth noting that the reviews with low quality are not equal to the review spam. A low-quality review may be caused by the reviewer's experience, education, etc. Such opinion information should be treated according to the application requirement, rather than filtered out directly.

Not all contents in text contain opinion. Opinion information extraction focuses on identifying and extracting the subjective contents from text. A basic task on this topic is to determine whether a document contains opinions or identify which contents in document contain opinions. After Mihalcea and his colleagues analyzed some research projects [Andreevskaia and Bergler (2006); Esuli and Sebastiani (2006a); Takamura *et al.* (2006)], they reported that distinguishing the subjective contents from the objective ones in documents is more difficult than identifying opinion types in Ref. [Mihalcea *et al.* (2007)]. Besides the documents, some previous works on subjective object detection focused on a finer grain of sentences and entities such as Refs. [Hatzivassiloglou and Wiebe (2000, 2005); Pang and Lee (2004); Hatzivassiloglou and Wiebe (2004)]. The opinion entities can be opinion holders, opinion targets, and opinion words. Opinion holder indicates who expresses the opinion. Extracting opinion holder is also an important task. In general, a opinion holder is a named entity like name and organization. Thus, the opinion holders can be extracted by the techniques of Name Entity Recognition (NER). Opinion target is the object that user opinions express on. For example, the product attributes always are the opinion target in product reviews. Opinion words are the words and phrases users use to express their opinions, which are often regarded as the adjectives and verbs.

Opinion identification is to identify what types of opinion expressed in opinion text, which can be treated as a classification problem. This work can be done at different granularities. For the case of document level, a document will be classified as one of the predefined categories according to its overall sentiment orientation. Most works on opinion classification focus on two opposite opinion categories (positive, negative) [Turney (2002); Pang *et al.* (2002); Lin *et al.* (2012c); Tan *et al.* (2011); Pan *et al.* (2010)] and three categories (positive, neutral, negative) [Feng *et al.* (2011); Barbosa and Feng (2010, 2011); Wilson *et al.* (2005)]. Of course, we can divide user opinions into multiple types by different sentiment intensity levels such as positive, weak positive, neutral, weak negative, and negative. However, with the increase in type number, it is difficult for user to determine which category a document belongs to really. In some cases, the opinion targets need to be refined. For example, user can comment the appearance, screen, and power consumption in a review on cellphone.

The traditional text retrieval techniques focus on string similarity. With more opinion-rich user-generated contents appearing on the Web, the retrieval techniques related to opinions become basic requirements. Opinion retrieval needs to search the documents meeting the topic relevance as well as the opinion relevance. Such systems seek the documents related to query topic at first. Then the opinions expressed on the corresponding topic are identified. At last, the retrieval document are sorted according to the opinion score and the relevance score. Thus, opinion retrieval combines the traditional text retrieval techniques and the opinion analysis techniques, which is one of the basic functions of new search engines.

The results of opinion analysis need to be shown to users. If the opinion information is too much, it would take users much time to process them. For instance, user often cannot read all reviews on a popular product, since lots of user comment it. Opinion summarization induces and concludes the opinion information contained in reviews automatically. It can bring a concise manner to show users the information contained in original review set. By this way, users can process the dominant information conveniently. Opinion classification can be treated as a coarse grained opinion summarization since it can determine the overall opinion of a document. However, the potential consumers would prefer to know the main features of a product. Thus, opinion summarization on product attributes would meet the users' requirements better.

Opinion analysis covers all the processes from collecting data to showing analysis results. In the process of opinion analysis, it needs to apply the techniques on information retrieval, machine learning, data mining, and natural language processing. Thus, opinion analysis is an interdisciplinary study field.

1.2 The application prospects and challenges

Online reviews have the features of great variety and massive scale, which provide rich data for opinion analysis. Therefore, opinion analysis can play an important role in many applications, and it possesses great potentials and long-term developing prospects.

(1) Business decision and review analysis. Business intelligence targets at aiding enterprise to make decisions by integrating, presenting, and analyzing relative data. The conventional investigation ways encounter the problems of heavy workload and difficult information collection. However, there are lots of reviews on products, which express a wealth of useful information such as the experiences and opinions of users. The manufacturers can make decisions

and improve quality of product based on these information to promote the customer satisfaction. Now, opinion analysis has been applied in practical applications. For example, the OpinionFinder system [Wilson *et al.* (2005)] can identify the subjective sentences and extract the sentiment information contained in sentences automatically. Yao *et al.* have developed an opinion analysis system to mine and summary the Chinese automobile reviews on sorts of auto brands [Yao *et al.* (2006)].

(2) Retrieval service based on users' opinions. Many retrieve results wanted by users are relative to the opinions, such as "Which film is the most interesting one in this year?," "Which one is the best place in Shanghai?." For such queries, the search engines need not only to retrieve the content-relevant pages, but also identify the opinion expressed by the opinion holders. Such queries also appear in Question Answering systems, and the opinion analysis is essential for such applications in these systems [Lita *et al.* (2005); Somasundaran *et al.* (2007); Stoyanov *et al.* (2005)]. For the issues on definitions, if the answers contain others' opinions on definitions, they would be easier to be understood by users [Lita *et al.* (2005)].

(3) Government intelligence. The social networking sites, such as online forums and microblogs, are important ways for users to obtain news and express their opinions, and are also an important platform for government agencies to obtain public opinions. Detecting pubic opinions on special events and policies quickly is useful for government to raise response speed, to make effective solutions, to restrict scale of negative effect, to promote reputation of government, and to maintain social stability. For another, some political events could be predicted by analyzing the opinions existed in Web data. For example, Kim successfully predicts the result of US presidential election by analyzing Web news reviews on election [Kim and Hovy (2007)].

(4) Web advertising. The huge count of network users provide a new chance for advertising. The traditional advertising shows same advertisement contents to all users, which makes poor effectiveness. However, Web users' profiles and requirements can be predicted by their browsing history, posted contents, and so on. Thus, it makes directional delivery possible, namely, it provides personalized advertisements for users. But the base of such applications is to identify users' preference.

(5) Precise recommendation service. The browsed or posted contents of a user can reflect what contents the user cares about and what are users' preference, hence user profile can come into being through these information. Based on these information, advertising user with appropriate products, news and services will achieve good effectiveness.

(6) E-audiobooks. Many books and novels contain rich sentiment. If the sentiment expressed in each sentence can be identified correctly, so as to adjust
the corresponding tone and speed, it would improve the expressiveness and
infectivity of texts, and would arouse audiences' resonance.

There are some Web sites providing opinion analysis functions, which are
shown in Table 1.1. The second column indicates the languages supported by
the system. In the third column, each capital letter indicates a granularity. The
forth column indicates what categories the system supports. For example, The
"3, $[-1,1]$" in second line means AlchemyAPI provides two forms of opinion
category. The first form is three categories (positive, neural, negative). The second
form is a real number locating in -1 and 1.

Table 1.1   Some Web sites proving opinion analysis functions

Name	Language[a]	Granularity[b]	Opinion category	Website
AlchemyAPI	en	D, S, E	3, $[-1,1]$	www.alchemyapi.com
Lymbix	en	D, S	8, $[-10,10]$	www.lymbix.com
Musicmetric	en	D	5	www.musicmetric.com
OpinionCrawl	en, fr, de, es	S	3	www.opinioncrawl.com
Opendover	en	E	3,$[-9,9]$	www.opendover.nl
Repustate	en, fr, de, es, ar	D, E	$[-1,1]$	www.repustate.com
Semantria	en, fr, de, es, pt	D, E	$[-1,1]$	www.semantria.com
sentiment140	en	D	3	www.sentiment140.com
SentimentAnalyzer	en, de, fr	D, E	3, $[-1,1]$	www.sentimentanalyzer
SentiRate	en	D, S	11	www.sentirate.com
Sentimetrix	en, fr, it, zh, ru, es	D	3, $[-1,1]$	www.sentimetrix.com
Uclassify	en	D	2, $[-1,1]$	www.uclassify.com
ViraHeat	en	D	2	www.viralheat.com
Wingify	en	D	$[0,1]$	www.wingify.com

[a] en = English, fr = French, de = German, es = Spanish, ar = Arabic, pt = Portuguese, it = Italian, zh = Chinese,
ru = Russian
[b] D = Document, S = Sentence, E = Entity

Although there are lots of works on opinion analysis, many areas still need to
be explored. At the same time, the development of Web applications brings new
chances and challenges for this field. Overall, main challenges can be summarized
as follows.

(1) The complexity of sentiment expression. Sentiment can often be expressed in a more subtle manner, making it difficult to be identified by any sentences or document's terms when they are considered in isolation [Pang and Lee (2008)]. Identifying such opinions is very difficult. For example, a movie review like "I should stay at home." could express a negative sentiment, though this review does not contain any negative words.

(2) The dependency of opinion expression. User opinion's expressions are influenced by his/her own education, cultural background, and experiences. Different users can have different opinions on the same sentence. Even for the same sentence written by a user, the opinions could depend on the context or the feeling at the moment. A word expresses different sentiment for different analyzed domains. For an instance, "predictable" expresses the positive opinion for electronics, while it is not desired for a novel.

(3) Ground truth is difficult to acquire. Labeling samples is a difficult task in opinion analysis, since it is subjective. For the same review, different readers could have inconsistent understanding. Thus, it is hard to obtain the ground truth to verify the effectiveness of proposed identification techniques.

(4) High noise and disunity text formats. Now social network platforms are the main way to collect data on user opinions. The openness of such platforms makes text formats inconsistent. At the same time, such data has high noise, since they are generated by users. How to integrate the data from different sources and reduce the noise, is an important and difficult problem.

(5) Huge data volume and fast update. The volume of contents containing user opinions is huge, and these contents are updated fast. So it is very urgent and necessary to store and retrieve these massive data efficiently.

The rest of this book is structured as follows. Chapter 2 outlines the related works on opinion analysis. Chapter 3 introduces some preliminaries, which includes review presentations for machine learning, single classifier methods, the commonly used evaluation metrics for opinion analysis and some potential datasets. Chapter 4 presents how to use sentiment information of terms to improve the performance of opinion analysis. Firstly, the limitation of traditional feature presentation methods for opinion analysis tasks is presented. And then a new feature presentation method is proposed, which integrates the sentiment information and contributions of features. A series of opinion classification experiments based on this new presentation method are carried on for different domains. Chapter 5 focuses on the problem of classifier selection together with the problem of how to improve the performance on opinion analysis based on available classifiers. A three-phase ensemble learning framework is proposed, in which a set of classifiers are chosen based on the accuracies and diversity. To assemble the chosen classifiers, an algorithm based on *stacking* technique is devised. At last, the experiment results are analyzed and discussed. Chapter 6 explores the Combinatorial Explosion Problem of classifiers. This chapter proposes a greedy algorithm for classifier selection, which proves to be 2-approximation. This solution is compared with multiple existing methods for opinion analysis in different domains. And the effectiveness of the proposed method is discussed. Chapter 7 introduces our works on opinion spam detection. The fake reviews can be highlighted based on review contents and the reviewer behaviors. Two supervised methods and a threshold-based method are applied to identify review spam. At last, Chapter 8 concludes our works.

Chapter 2

Related works

Opinion analysis for online reviews has attracted much attention in recent years, since it has significant applicable and research value. There are much previous work focusing on this filed, which involved many study topics like review quality evaluation, opinion identification, opinion information extraction, opinion spam detection, and so on. In this chapter, we introduce some related works in this field.

2.1 Quality control on reviews

Online review is one kind of typical user-generated contents, which contains rich user opinions. At the same time, it has the features of large volume, speed, exchange interaction and the influence of the range. Thus, reviews are often treated as primary objects by researchers in opinion analysis field. On the other side, the quality of reviews cannot be guaranteed because of the network openness and the user diversity. Therefore, evaluating review quality is an important task before analyzing and utilizing them. In the following subsections, we present related techniques and ways of quality control for reviews.

2.1.1 *The policies on encouraging users to write good reviews*

In the phase of generating reviews, the websties proving review functions can guide users to prefer to write true and good reviews by restricting some inappropriate behaviors and affecting the psychologies of users. Many e-commerce sites only allow the users, who have purchased products in the sites, to review products. In some senses, this way can ensure that the review presents user's true experiences. On the other hand, it can raise the costs of making review spam. However, it would keep some potential high quality review back by this way though it can reduce the amount of low quality reviews and review spam. Besides, most websites make restrictions on review length, since reviews are too short to carry information on product features and user opinions. Of course, if reviews are too long, they would contain redundant or useless information.

Most websites allow users to vote on the helpfulness of review, and treat the votes as a primary indicator on evaluating reviewer's contribution. Users would be given material rewards or moral encouragement according to their contributions. For example, the top k reviewers' names will be put in a conspicuous place of the webpage, and the users will be awarded different titles. Such ways would make users prefer to write good reviews subconsciously. In addition, users can report review spam to site administrators, and they also can comment existing reviews. The results generated by these approaches, like helpfulness and reporting, not only help websites to maintain the review quality, but also can be treated as the potential ground truth in some studies on review analysis. Some websites also provide user guide to help them to write high-quality reviews. Table 2.1 shows some policies on encouraging users to make good reviews in some famous websites.[1]

Table 2.1   The common ways on review quality control in some famous websites

Name	After purchasing	Length[a]	Helpfulness vote	Reporting	User honour	Writing guide
Amazon	√	$L \geq 20$ W	√	√	—	√
eBay	—	$100\ C \leq L \leq 3500$ C	√	√	√	√
TripAdvisor	—	$L \geq 200$ C	√	√	√	—
IMDB	—	$L \geq 5$ W	√	—	√	√
Taobao	√	$0 \leq L \leq 500$ W	√	—	√	√
Dianping	—	$50\ W \leq L \leq 2000$ W	√	√	√	√
Douban	—	$0 \leq L \leq 140$ W	√	—	—	√
Dangdang	√	$0 \leq L \leq 3000$ W	√	—	√	√

[a] W = Word, C = Char, L = Length

2.1.2   *Quality evaluation of reviews*

Review quality is a subject concept. The evaluation criteria are different for various users. The book reviews were studied in Ref. [Tsur and Rappoport (2009)], in which the authors reported that a good/helpful book review should provide readers sufficient information on book topic, plot, writing style, background, and so on.

---

[1]The websites are listed as following from top to bottom in first column of Table 2.1: www.amazon.com, www.ebay.com, www.tripadvisor.com, www.imdb.com, www.taobao.com, www.dianping.com, www.douban.com, www.dangdang.com

In this book, we focus on product reviews, and not just on book reviews. Thus, the good/high-quality/helpful reviews can be defined as those that can describe product attributes and performances specifically, and help potential users to make appropriate decisions.

The target of review quality evaluation is to quantify review's quality in a predetermined range or to classify/rank reviews according to their quality. The statistics on review helpfulness vote is a main way to evaluate review quality in most websites. However, such evaluation way encounters the problem of voting process's fairness. This fairness could come from users as well as reviews. If a user has a prejudice against a product brand, this prejudice would affect his/her vote. Therefore, the votes coming from biased users should be assigned with low weight when the helpfulness vote is treated as the review quality evaluation criterion, by which such users' influence would be reduced [Mishra and Rastogi (2012)]. For the vote unfairness on review helpfulness, the causes were summarized as following in Ref. [Liu *et al.* (2007)]:

(1) Users prefer to vote for helpfulness rather than uselessness.
(2) The reviews with high number of votes would be more likely to receive votes.
(3) The reviews appeared early would receive more helpfulness votes.

The review quality is affected by a number of factors [Kim and Movy (2006); Lu *et al.* (2010); Liu *et al.* (2008); P O'Mahony and Smyth (2009); Ghose and Ipeirotis (2007); Zhang and Varadarajan (2006); Otterbacher (2009); Danescu-Niculescu-Mizil *et al.* (2009)]. Thus, We can classify or rank reviews' quality according to these factors. In terms of review contents, the factors involve mainly:

(1) Syntactic features. Such features focus on the numbers or proportions of various Part-Of-Speech (POS) words, the presence or absence of emotion verbs, exclamations, comparative/superlative adjectives or adverbs, interrogatives, and so on.
(2) Semantics features. Such feature could be the numbers of subjective or objective words and sentences, the words or sentences with positive/negative sentiment, the number of product features contained in review, and so on.
(3) Meta features in reviews. Such as user rating, average rating of product, the different between user rating and average rating, writing time of review, helpfulness votes, and so on.
(4) Statistic features. The number of words/sentences/paragraphs contained in review, the proportions of capital letter/litter letter, the number of hyperlinks, and so on.
(5) Readability. This index can be evaluated by the number of spelling mistakes,

the length of review, the average length of sentences, and some readability indicators like Automated Readability Index (ARI) [Smith and Senter (1962)], Simple Measure of Gobbledygook score (SMOG) [McLahghlin1 (1969)], Gunning-Fog [Gunning (1968)], and so on.

(6) Similarity features. This types of features try to compare content similarity, the indicators include Jaccard similarity, Consin similarity, Kullback-leibler Divergence, and so on.

In terms of reviewer, the factors affecting review quality contain mainly:

(1) The average rating of reviewer's ratings.
(2) The flags reflecting whether a reviewer registered his/her true name, whether a reviewer has honor medals. The number of his/ her reviews. The average number and standard deviation of all reviewers.
(3) The average helpfulness vote of a reviewers, and its difference with average helpfulness vote of all reviewers. This difference could show the rating habit of the reviewer.
(4) Social features. If there are social network among reviewers, the reviewers' relationships can be modeled by graph. Such features contain the vertex's in-degree, out-degree, PageRank score [Brin and Page (1998)], and so on.
(5) The reviewer's experiences. The quality of review is often affected by reviewer's experiences. For example, the reviewers, who enjoy science fictions, should be good at writing reviews on films like *The Matrix Revolutions* and *Star Wars*. Thus, such factors should be considered for the prediction model of review quality evaluation.

On the basis of these factors, prediction on review quality can be often treated either as a classification problem [P O'Mahony and Smyth (2009); Liu *et al.* (2007); Siersdorfer *et al.* (2010); Weimer *et al.* (2007)] or a regression problem [Kim and Movy (2006); Liu *et al.* (2008); Ghose and Ipeirotis (2007); Zhang and Varadarajan (2006); Otterbacher (2009); Mudambi and Schuff (2010)]. Besides these two kinds of methods, there are other ways to evaluate review quality. For example, Tsur and Rappoport considered that a good book review should provide readers with adequate information on the book's topic, plot, writing backgrounds, and so on. They proposed a threshold-based approach to find the most helpful book reviews in Ref. [Tsur and Rappoport (2009)], which is based on a constructed dictionary of dominant terms constituting the core of a virtual optimal review. Recently, Tang *et al.* exploited context awareness to infer unknown helpfulness ratings automatically, where they extracted four types of social contexts and proposed a Context-Aware helpfulness rating Prediction framework (CAP) [Tang *et al.* (2013)].

For different types of products, the factors affecting review quality are also various. Nelson divided products into two categories: the experience goods and the search goods [Nelson (1970)]. An experience good is a product or service where product characteristics, such as quality or price, are difficult to observe in advance, but these characteristics can be ascertained upon consumption, such as movies and music. A search good refers to that with features and characteristics easily evaluated before purchase. After Mudambi and Schuff studied and analyzed the reviews from Amazon.com across six products, they reported that reviews with extreme ratings are less helpful than reviews with moderate ratings for experience goods in Ref. [Mudambi and Schuff (2010)]. Moreover, they found review depth has a positive effect on helpfulness of review for both product types, but it has a greater positive effect for search goods than for experience goods.

2.1.3 *Review spam detection*

Driven by quick profits, some users write false reviews deliberately to mislead potential consumers. Such reviews deviating from truth are often called review spam. In order to hide the spammers' identities and achieve their goal of misleading consumers, they always try to make their reviews look like the normal ones. Thus, it is not easy for review readers to identify review spam. Two reviews on different products from Amazon are shown in Figs. 2.1(a)[2] and (b)[3], which are written by two reviewer IDs. If we read these two reviews solely, we find nothing unusual. But when we bring them together, we find that they are almost identical. We can infer that the first one is a fake review at least, since it is posted later than the other one. Besides that, Fig. 2.1(a) shows that all of 16 readers, who have commented the first suspicious review, consider the fake review to be helpful for them, which means many users are deceived by it. Therefore, this difficulty will make the labeled samples insufficient and the effect evaluation of review spam detection, which is one of the challenges for review spam detection.

Review spam emerges as result of unfair competition. For example, a merchant could hire spammers to write false positive reviews for them to improve their popularity. On the other side, they could also hire spammers to write false negative reviews for damaging their rivals' popularity. Such reviews would seriously affect the healthy competition in e-commerce environment, and damage the interests of consumers. Therefore, review spam should be filtered out before

---

[2]http://www.amazon.com/gp/cdp/member-reviews/A2GZFZNFDRSYHV/ref=cm_cr_pr_auth_rev? ie=UTF8&sort_by=MostRecentReview

[3]http://www.amazon.com/gp/cdp/member-reviews/A2TUHWW5DLTN4U/ref=cm_cr_pr_auth_rev? ie=UTF8&sort_by=MostRecentReview

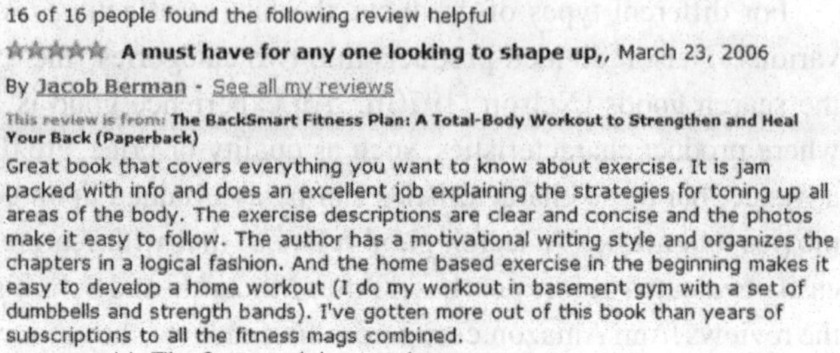

16 of 16 people found the following review helpful

☆☆☆☆☆ **A must have for any one looking to shape up,**, March 23, 2006

By <u>Jacob Berman</u> - <u>See all my reviews</u>

This review is from: **The BackSmart Fitness Plan: A Total-Body Workout to Strengthen and Heal Your Back (Paperback)**

Great book that covers everything you want to know about exercise. It is jam packed with info and does an excellent job explaining the strategies for toning up all areas of the body. The exercise descriptions are clear and concise and the photos make it easy to follow. The author has a motivational writing style and organizes the chapters in a logical fashion. And the home based exercise in the beginning makes it easy to develop a home workout (I do my workout in basement gym with a set of dumbbells and strength bands). I've gotten more out of this book than years of subscriptions to all the fitness mags combined.

(a) The first suspicious review

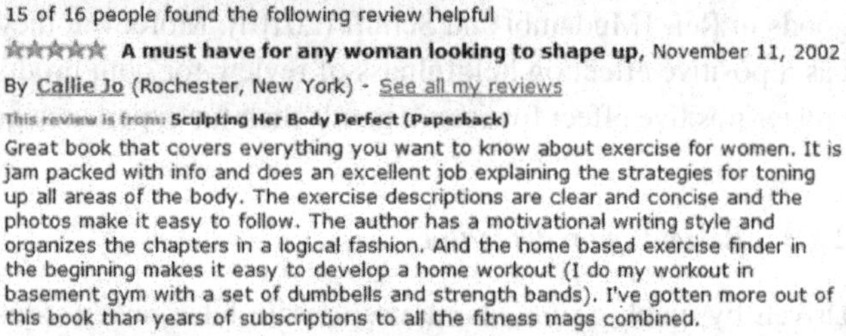

15 of 16 people found the following review helpful

☆☆☆☆☆ **A must have for any woman looking to shape up,** November 11, 2002

By <u>Callie Jo</u> (Rochester, New York) - <u>See all my reviews</u>

This review is from: **Sculpting Her Body Perfect (Paperback)**

Great book that covers everything you want to know about exercise for women. It is jam packed with info and does an excellent job explaining the strategies for toning up all areas of the body. The exercise descriptions are clear and concise and the photos make it easy to follow. The author has a motivational writing style and organizes the chapters in a logical fashion. And the home based exercise finder in the beginning makes it easy to develop a home workout (I do my workout in basement gym with a set of dumbbells and strength bands). I've gotten more out of this book than years of subscriptions to all the fitness mags combined.

(b) The second suspicious review

Fig. 2.1   Two suspicious review examples on Amazon

reviews are shown to consumers. The detection targets contain three main types as following:

(1) **Review spam**. Most prior works focus on detecting review spam. Jindal and Liu divided review spam into three categories in Ref. [Jindal and Liu (2007, 2008)]: the reviews containing false opinions on products, those not commenting on the product, but on the brand (or manufacturer or seller) and those without any opinions. They claimed that the first type of spam is more harmful than others, and detected such review spam based on the proposed 32 features. They treated the duplicates or near-duplicates of reviews as spam. Ott *et al.* analyzed the effectiveness of the POS tag, psycholinguistic features, and text features for spotting deceptive opinion spam based on Support Vector Machine (SVM), and they found that the combination of psycholinguistic features, and text features perform slightly better [Ott *et al.* (2011)]. Li *et al.* found review spam could be identified from two views [Li *et al.* (2011)]: review features and reviewer features. To exploit large amount of unlabeled samples, they applied a semi-supervised method, co-training, to identify review spam. Wu *et al.* proposed a method for detecting suspicious reviews in Ref. [Wu *et al.* (2010b)], because they found that deleting dishonest reviews

would distort the popularity rating. Xie *et al.* detected spam attacks launched by singleton reviews with bursts detection on three dimensions: rating, review number and ratio of single reviews [Xie *et al.* (2012)]. Wu *et al.* presented eight criterions in Ref. [Wu *et al.* (2010a)], which might be indicative of suspicious reviews. They evaluated two methods (singular value decomposition method and unsupervised Hedge algorithm) to integrate these criterions to produce an unified suspiciousness ranking. In summary, the features used for anti-review spam are shown as following.

- Review features. This type of features can be refined further as text features, sentiment features, and metadata features. The first one includes the occurrence frequencies of product brand, numbers, capital letters, the first/second person, similarity between detected review and others. The second one includes the ratio between subject words and objective words, the ratio between positive words and negative words, and so on. The last one includes the review length, the rating of review, the helpfulness votes, the review time, and so on.
- Reviewer features. This type of features describes personal information of reviewer, such as the number of his/her reviews, the presence or absence of reviewer's true name in his/her person description, and the reviewer's ranking. The behavior feature is another type of reviewer features, which contains the average rating of reviewer, the standard deviation of ratings, the difference among review numbers of the various brands, the rating difference among reviews on various brands, and so on.
- Product features. Such features include information on a product, such as the review number, the standard deviation of ratings, the average rating, the price, and the sales ranking.

(2) **Review spammer**. Compared with review spam detection, spammer detection is more difficult, since spammer might have the dual capacity. In other words, a spammer would probably write normal reviews. However, some behaviors would show cues to highlight the spammers. Lim *et al.* devised an aggregated behavior scoring methods to rank reviewers according to the degree of suspicious behaviors in Ref. [Lim *et al.* (2010)]. In Ref. [Wang *et al.* (2012)], the relationships among all reviewers, reviews and stores were captured via constructing a review graph, and then an iterative computational model was used to identify suspicious reviewers. Lee *et al.* deployed some special accounts, called social honeypots, on MySpace[4] and Twitter[5] to

---

[4]https://myspace.com
[5]www.twitter.com

collect profiles of suspicious accounts, they applied the classifiers trained on spammers' profiles and normal users' profiles to uncover the social spammers [Lee *et al.* (2010)].

(3) **The group of review spammers**. In general, a small amount of review spam would have little effect. When a group of spammers join together to write fake reviews to promote or demote a set of target products in a short time window, it will have a great harmful influence. Mukherjee *et al.* aimed at detecting spammer group; they firstly applied frequent pattern mining to find candidate groups; and designed eight criterias to estimate candidate groups. At last, they ranked the candidates by SVM rank [Mukherjee *et al.* (2011)]. Their further study [Mukherjee *et al.* (2012)] extended the criterias with four individual spam behavior indicators, and designed a ranking algorithm called GSRank based on the inter-relationships among products, groups, and group members.

2.2 Opinion information extracting

As discussed in Chapter 1, the core opinion objects refer to opinion holder, opinion target, and opinion expression. There are lots of works focusing on the extraction of opinion targets, which are important because without knowing the targets, the opinions expressed in a sentence or document are of limited use. For opinion analysis on product reviews, opinion target are often product's attributes (aspects/features). For example, in the opinion sentence "I don't like the screen of this camera," *screen* is the opinion target. Without this information, we will lose most of value of this opinion. Extraction of opinion target is a difficult task in opinion analysis. The common methods include associated rule mining [Hu and Liu (2004a)], dependency analysis [Zhuang *et al.* (2006)], pattern mining [Kobayashi *et al.* (2007)], rule-based methods [Poria *et al.* (2014)], sequence labeling [Stoyanov and Cardie (2008)], and so on.

Nouns and noun phrases are often treated as product aspect candidates. Hu and Liu mined frequent nouns and noun phrases by the Apriori algorithm, and removed the uninteresting and redundant feature candidates with a *Compactness pruning* process and a *Redundancy pruning* process in Ref. [Hu and Liu (2004b)]. In the first process, those candidate features whose words did not appear together were pruned. In the second process, the redundant features containing single words were removed by a *p-support* threshold. Popescu and Etzioni proposed an algorithm to determine whether a noun–noun phrase was a feature by computing the PMI score between phrase and class-specific discriminators through a Web search [Popescu and Etzioni (2007)]. Topic Model can also be used to identify product feature. Stoyanov and Cardie clustered opinions sharing the same target together, and trained a classifier to predict if two opinions are on same target in Ref. [Stoyanov and Cardie (2008)]. Mei *et al.* proposed a probabilistic mixture model called Topic-Sentiment Mixture (TSM) to model and extract the multiple targets and sentiments on different weblog data sets in Ref. [Mei *et al.* (2007)]. Yi and Niblack developed a set of feature term extraction heuristics and selection algorithms for extracting a feature term from product reviews in Ref. [Yi and Niblack (2005)]. At first, they extracted a noun phrase with the Beginning define Base Noun Phrase heuristics. Then, they selected a feature term from the noun phrase using a likelihood score.

Adjectives are the words users often use to express their opinions. In order to acquire lots of opinion words, some previous works expanded the existing directions like WordNet with seed words selected manually [Hatzivassiloglou and Wiebe (2005); Kim and Hovy (2006)]. Such dictionary-based methods are easy to implement, but they depended on the seed words. Moreover, Kanayama and Nasukawa proposed a corpora-based approach to extract the opinion words in Ref. [Kanayama and Nasukawa (2006)]. They used clause level context coherency to find candidates, then used a statistical estimation method to determine whether the candidates are appropriate opinion words. This method for finding candidates would have low recall, if the occurrences of seed words in the corpora are infrequent or unknown opinion words have no known opinions in contexts. Besides, the statistical estimation can be unreliable if the corpus is small, it is a common problem for statistical approaches.

For opinion analysis on reviews, opinion targets and opinion words are often considered together. There are two types of methods on collective extraction of opinion target and opinion word: the window-based nearest neighbor method [Hu and Liu (2004b); Wang and Wang (2008)] and the syntactic pattern-based method [Qiu *et al.* (2011); Popescu and Etzioni (2007)]. The former has a relatively low extraction precision, since the span of words is limited by the size of the predetermined window. The latter need to parse words' dependencies at first. However, user reviews always contain irregular contents, such as the errors of syntax, spelling and punctuation. Thus, the parse results always contain some errors, which would affect the performance of extraction. Although the extraction precision can be improved by setting more sophisticated 'syntactic patterns, it would lead to a relatively poor recall. Qiu *et al.* proposed an approach, called *double propagation*, to extract opinion words (or targets) iteratively using known and extracted (in previous iterations) opinion words and targets through the identification of syntactic relations [Qiu *et al.* (2011)].

Moreover, the collective extraction of opinion word and opinion target can also be treated as a sequence labeling problem. Some classic sequence labeling models can be used to construct the extractors, such as Conditional Random Fields [Li *et al.* (2010a)] and Hidden Markov Model [Jin and Ho (2009)]. But this type of methods require labeled samples to train extraction models. The process of labeling samples is time consuming and laborious. For another, if training samples are not enough or the domain of samples is different from that of extracted samples, the extraction performance would be affected significantly. Recently, Liu *et al.* presented a novel approach for extracting opinion targets and opinion words from online reviews in Ref. [Liu *et al.* (2014)], in which the collective extraction of opinion targets and opinion words is performed by a co-ranking process. They modeled semantic relations and opinion words over a bipartite graph firstly, in which nouns are treated as opinion target candidates, whereas adjectives and verbs are treated as opinion word candidates. A co-ranking algorithm is proposed to perform candidate confidence estimation secondly, which is based on three random walks on different subgraphs.

2.3 Opinion classification on different granularities

Opinion classification for online reviews targets at identifying the overall sentiment orientation expressed in text. According to the text's granularity, opinion classification can be implemented at different levels, such as word-level, document-level, and product attribute-level. The sentiment of words and phases can reflect the overall sentiment orientation of document, and the product attributes can be included in multiple documents. Thus, the sentiment classifications of these three granularities are intimately related.

2.3.1 *The word-level opinion classification*

The methods on word-level opinion analysis can be divided into two groups: the dictionary-based and the statistics-based. The former uses the relations, such as synonym and antonym, of some seeds and other words to predict the word's sentiment. The latter predicts the word's sentiment by using the words' co-occur patterns and syntax clues.

Sentiment dictionary is the most intuitive way to identify word's sentiment. The classes of opinions are determined by the appliances commonly, they can be categorized into two classes (positive or negative) or three classes (positive or neutral or negative) in most cases. Of course, we can apply more sentiment classes according to sentiment strength. The SentiWordNet [Esuli and Sebastiani (2006b)] is a general sentiment dictionary,[6] which is developed by Esuli *et al.* in

---

[6]The current version of SentiWordNet is 3.0. http://sentiwordnet.isti.cnr.it/

University di Padoval based on the WordNet [Miller *et al.* (1990)]. This sentiment dictionary describes each word from two dimensions [Baccianella *et al.* (2010)], as shown in Fig. 2.2. The location of a word in this triangle means its sentiment orientation. In the horizontal direction, if a word locates at the right area, it prefers to express stronger negative sentiment. In the vertical direction, a word locating at the upper area will tend to be more objective.

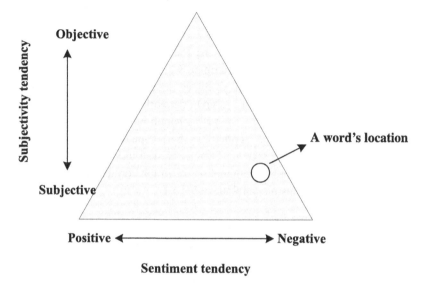

Fig. 2.2 The graphical representation adopted by SentiWordNet for representing the opinion-related properties of a term sense

The main disadvantage of sentiment dictionary-based methods is that much words' sentiment is domain-depended, namely, a word could express various sentiment in different domains. For example, the word "predictable" is positive for describing electronic products. But when we say a movie or book is predictable, we would want to express negative sentiment. Lu *et al.* converted the sentiment identification problem into a linear programming problem based on four sources (the general sentiment dictionary, review's rating, general dictionary and some syntax rules), and constructed a domain and attribute-sensitive sentiment dictionary [Lu *et al.* (2011)]. A word's sentiment score can be determined by the word, its attribute and domain, which locates in $[-1, 1]$. According to this score, the word's sentiment orientation can be predicted. For example, for the printer reviews, the word "high" expresses positive sentiment in their dictionary when it describes the quality, and expresses negative sentiment for describing the noise.

Miller *et al.* developed a cognitive linguistics-based English dictionary Word-Net[7] in Princeton University [Miller *et al.* (1990)]. Besides the meaning of each word, it also provides a synonym network of words. Although WordNet does not clearly indicate words' sentiment, the word's synonyms are the good clue to identify its sentiment. Kim and Hovy manually selected a small set of seed words with specified sentiment (such as *good* and *bad*) firstly. And then, they used WordNet to search seed words' synonyms and antonyms, and labeled the synonyms' sentiment as the same to the seeds', labeled the antonyms opposite to the seeds'. By this way, the seed set is expanded. For a word's sentiment label, they turned to evaluate the sentiment of word's synonyms and antonyms in the expanded seed set, and used the ratio of them to determine word's sentiment [Kim and Hovy (2006)]. Godbole *et al.* treated the words as nodes, the synonym relations of words as edges, and constructed a synonym network [Bautin *et al.* (2008)]. A word's sentiment is determined by the path's length between word and seed, as shown in Fig. 2.3. Kamps *et al.* applied the shortest path to predict word's sentiment polarity in Ref. [Kamps *et al.* (2004)]. Hassan used the Markov random walk model to evaluate words' sentiment on the graph constructed by words' relationship in WordNet [Hassan and Radev (2010)].

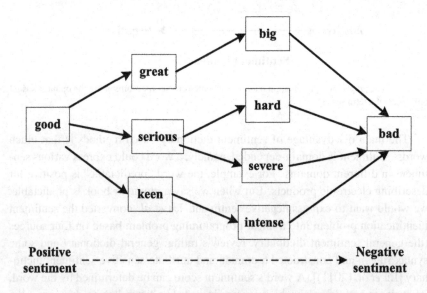

Fig. 2.3   Four synonym paths with 3 hops from "Good to Bad"

---

[7]The newest versions of WordNet are 2.1 for Windows and 3.0 for Unix/Linux/Solaris/ect. respectively. http://wordnet.princeton.edu/

The dictionary-based methods are easy to implement, but they depend on the quality and quantity of seed words. At the same time, the prediction accuracy is limited due to the polysemy. To reduce the influence of polysemous words, some researchers used glosses in WordNet to support word's sentiment identification [Andreevskaia and Bergler (2006); Su and Markert (2009); Esuli and Sebastiani (2005)]. On the other hand, for other languages, the resources are not as rich as those for English. Some works proposed to translate the WordNet to other languages for different applications [Mihalcea *et al.* (2007)], but such translating process could change words' sentiment polarities.

Besides dictionaries, some syntax clues can also be used to predict word's sentiment. Hatzicassiloglou and McKeown explored the problem of adjective sentiment identification in Ref. [Hatzivassiloglou and McKeown (1997)], they firstly labeled some seeds' sentiment labels, and then they applied conjunction-based rules to determine adjective's sentiment. For example, a seed word connects to a word by "and" and "or", then word's sentiment prefers to be same to the seed's. However, two adjectives connected by "but" always express the opposite sentiment. They labeled manually 1336 adjectives including 657 positive ones and 679 negative ones firstly. And then, they used these labeled seeds and such conjunction rules to predict the sentiment of 2.1 million adjectives in Wall Street Journal in 1987. They reported that the prediction accuracy was 97%. However, the weakness of this method is that it relies on the conjunction relation of adjectives.

Turney identified word's polarity with an unsupervised learning method in Ref. [Turney (2002)]. He measured word's point-wise mutual information (PMI) with some seeds like "excellent" and "poor," the calculation formulae is shown as follows:

$$PMI(word_1, word_2) = \log_2 \frac{P(w_1 \& w_2)}{P(W_1) * P(W_2)}. \qquad (2.1)$$

Here, $P(w_i)$ is the probability that word w_i occur, $P(w_1 \& w_2)$ is the probability that word w_1 and word w_2 co-occur. The ratio between $P(w_1 \& w_2)$ and $P(w_1)P(w_2)$ is a measure of the degree of statical dependence between words. To estimate PMI value, he used *near* operator of the AltaVista search engine[8] to search the instance pages. The AltaVisa *near* operator constrains the search to documents that contain the words within ten words of one another, in either order. Based on the PMI value, the Semantic Orientation of a phrase is calculated as follows:

$$SO(phase) = PMI(phrase, ``excellent") - PMI(phrase, ``poor"). \qquad (2.2)$$

This method is time consuming, since it requires to access the Web. Gamon and Aue improved Turney's method further in Ref. [Gamon and Aue (2005)],

---

[8]www.altavista.com

they assumed that two words with opposite sentiment would not co-occur in a sentence. This assumption made the word's sentiment prediction more reliable in their experiments. Moreover, Martineau identified the word's sentiment orientation by calculating the ratio of counts it occurred in negative documents and in positive documents respectively [Martineau *et al.* (2009)]. We used the words' mutual information with sentiment labels to measure sentiment score, which will be discussed in detail in Chapter 4.

2.3.2 *The document-level opinion classification*

Opinion analysis at document-level tries to identify the overall sentiment orientation of a document, which can be treated as a classification problem or regression problem. No matter what type of problems it falls in, when the machine learning methods are used to handle such tasks, there are always three basic factors needed determining: feature template, feature function, and classification algorithm. The former means what type of features will be used to model documents. The feature function maps each feature into a special value. And the classification algorithms like NaiveBayes, maximum entropy and SVM are effective for sentiment classification in many previous works. We will outline the related works based on these three factors.

In the bag-of-words framework, the n-gram, such as unigram, bigram, and trigram, is applied for opinion analysis commonly, which is made up of n continuous words. For example, each word in the sentence "This match works well" is a unigram, and the bigrams include "This match," "match works," and "works well". Pang *et al* compared different feature types (unigram, bigram, POS, adjectives, and the mixture of unigram and bigram, etc.) according to weighting functions and classification methods in movie reviews, they reported the SVM with unigram and presence achieved the highest accuracy (82.9%) in Ref. [Pang *et al.* (2002)]. However, Cui *et al.* reported in Ref. [Cui *et al.* (2006)] that when the amount of training samples is small, the unigram would achieve the good performance, but with the amount of training samples increasing, the n-gram ($n > 3$) would play more and more important role in sentiment classification. In Ref. [Matsumoto *et al.* (2005)], Matsumoto *et al.* expanded the features with frequent word sub-sequences and dependency sub-trees, which improved the classification performance. Emoticons are often used to express individual sentiment, thus they are treated as a type of features for analyzing the sentiment of contents on social website like Twitter[9] [Alm *et al.* (2005); Go *et al.* (2009)]. Agarwal *et al.* divided features into POS features and the others [Agarwal *et al.* (2011)], in which POS

---

[9]www.twitter.com

features stood for the features capturing statistics about POS of words. Yang and Pedersen made a comparative study on five feature selections including term selection based on document frequency, information gain, mutual information, χ^2 test and term strength in Ref. [Yang and Pedersen (1997)], they reported that the χ^2 test achieved the good effectiveness. It is worth mentioning that Suresh *et al.* used only the stopwords as the features for sentiment classification in Ref. [Venkatasubramanian *et al.* (2011)], in which their classification accuracies are also over 60%. This means stopwords can make an active function in sentiment classification. Thus, we will not omit stopwords in our experiments in this book.

Term frequency is used generally in sentiment classification [Pang *et al.* (2002); Lin *et al.* (2012b); Matsumoto *et al.* (2005)]. The classic *tfidf* schema was compared with its variants for opinion analysis [Paltoglou and Thelwall (2010)], and the authors emphasized that expressing sample vectors with emotional information via supervised methods was helpful for predicting sentiment polarity. Ref. [Martineau *et al.* (2009)] proposed a new feature function, $\Delta tfidf$, for sentiment polarity classification, by which the importance of discriminative terms could be identified and boosted. In Ref. [Lin *et al.* (2012b)], we applied mutual information to identify term's sentiment polarity and evaluated its contribution by term frequency, by which we achieved a good classification performance. Moreover, features can be weighted with some external resources, such as WordNet [Miller *et al.* (1990)]. But it does not always perform well by this way, since the sentiment of word is domain-aware.

SVM is one of the most frequently used classification algorithms in sentiment classification, and the former work [Pang *et al.* (2002)] showed that the SVM outperformed both NaiveByes and maximum entropy on movie reviews. Hassan and Radev applied Markov random walk model to a relatedness graph to estimate the polarity of a word in Ref. [Hassan and Radev (2010)]. Kamps constructed a network based on WordNet synonyms in Ref. [Kamps *et al.* (2004)], and they used the shortest path starting from a given word to the words 'good' and 'bad' to identify word's sentiment polarity. Based on phrases' semantic orientations, Turney calculated the average semantic orientation of phrases in given review and classify review as *recommended* if the average is positive and otherwise *not recommended* in Ref. [Turney (2002)]. Dave *et al.* used another unsupervised method to classify document d_i (where $d_i = f_1...f_n$) in Ref. [Dave *et al.* (2003)], in which they summed the scores of words in an unknown document and use the sigh of the total to determine a class:

$$class(d_i) = \begin{cases} C & eval(d_i) > 0 \\ C' & eval(d_i) < 0 \end{cases} \qquad (2.3)$$

where

$$eval\left(d_i = \sum_j \frac{p(f_i|C) - p(f_i|C')}{p(f_i|C) - p(f_i|C')} \right).$$

They determined $p(f_i|C)$, the normalized term frequency, by taking the number of times a feature f_i occurs in C and dividing it by the total number of token in C. A term's score is thus a measure of bias ranging from -1 to 1. Wei and Gulla applied hierarchical learning process with a defined sentiment ontology tree to label the sentiments in product reviews [Wei and Gulla (2010)]. In Ref. [Tan *et al.* (2011)], user's social relationships (follow relationship and @-convention) were used to analyze user's sentiment based on the principle of *homophily* without considering context information. Blitzer *et al.* applied an extend Structural Correspondence Learning (SCL) for a cross-domain sentiment classification problem, in which a key step was to select the pivot features to link the source and target domains [Blitzer *et al.* (2007)].

The ensemble technique can also be found in some literatures for sentiment classification. Li *et al.* applied Co-training to expand the training set based on reviewers' opinion and non-reviewers', and then they calculated the probabilities of samples' sentiment polarity predicted by two classifiers for Co-training and a classifier training on all training samples [Li *et al.* (2010b)]. Multiple predictions of a sample were integrated by multiplying these probabilities. Dasgupta and Vincent applied different types of learning methods including unsupervised learning, active learning, and transductive learning on sentiment classification in Ref. [Dasgupta and Ng (2009)]. The spectral clustering was used to label the reviews with explicit sentiment at first, the reviews with ambiguous sentiment were then chose by a active learning process to label manually. At last, all labeled reviews were used to train multiple transductive classifiers, and the final label of an unlabeled sample is generated by integrating multiple predictions made by these trained classifiers. In Refs. [Xia *et al.* (2011)] and [Lin *et al.* (2012c)], multiple feature sets and classification algorithms are integrated to synthesize a more accurate sentiment classification procedure, which have not explored the problem of how to select the member classifiers. We proposed a criteria for selecting member classifiers based on their accuracies and diversity in Ref. [Lin *et al.* (2012a)], but this method suffers the Combinatorial Explosion Problem, which is explored in Chapter 6.

2.3.3 *The attribute-level opinion classification*

For the reviews on products, readers may be more interested in users' opinion on products' attributes, such as the iPhone 5's battery. Identifying the sentiment on product attributes always involves three steps as following:

(1) Extracting product attributes.
(2) Identifying user's sentiment on corresponding product attributes.
(3) Summarizing different users' sentiment on each attribute.

Extracting product attributes can be implemented with some heuristic syntax rules, for example, product attributes are nouns or noun phrases in common. But it is clear that not all nouns or noun phrases are product attributes. In Ref. [Yi *et al.* (2003)], Yi *et al.* extracted product attributes from noun phrases appearing in reviews with three heuristic rules. Hu and Liu considered that nouns and noun phrases occurring in reviews frequently were likely to be product attributes in Ref. [Hu and Liu (2004b)]. They found product attribute candidates by frequent item set mining technique, and pruned with the rule-based methods to make the attributes extracted more accuracy. For example, for the "life" and the "battery life", the latter is remained only. Popescu and Etzioni divided attributes into the explicit attributes and the implicit ones, and implemented structure analysis of reviews with the MINIPAR system [Lin (2003)] in Ref. [Popescu and Etzioni (2007)]. And then, they calculated the PMI values of attributes and products with KnowItAll [Etzioni *et al.* (2005)] to determine product attributes. All of these methods above are unsupervised. In Ref. [Liu *et al.* (2005)], to extract product attributes, Liu *et al.* used the CBA system to mine the rules on attributes in review set with labeled attributes [Liu *et al.* (1998)].

Titov and Ryan treated the product attributes as latent topics in document collection in Ref. [Titov and McDonald (2008)]. They devised an improved topic model to mine latent opinion words on product attributes, and applied classification method to identify the users' sentiment on product attributes. The sentiment orientation prediction for product attributes can be implemented with above sentiment identification techniques at word-level or document-level. For example, Hu and Liu labeled 30 typical adjectives as the seeds, used words' relationship with their synonyms and antonyms in WorNet to determine users' sentiment on product attributes [Hu and Liu (2004a)].

The descriptions on attributions of a product could come from many reviews. Thus, if the summarization of the users' sentiment on product attributes are shown to users, it would be more convenient and comprehensive for users to know a product. The traditional text summary techniques can be divided into two groups: the extractive summarization and the abstractive summarization. The former extracts some important sentences or paragraphs from original texts to form a short text, such as Ref. [Chen *et al.* (2002); Gupta and Lehal (2009)]. The latter needs to define a template at first, and selects the most important information.

After such information is aggregated, they are filled in the template to generate a new summary text, such as Ref. [Erkan and Radev (2004); Hahn and Romacker (2001)]. However, for the summarization on product reviews, it is not adequate just summarizing at document level, since many potential customers and manufacturers would prefer to focus on users' opinions about the product attributes. Thus, summarizing reviewers' opinions according to product attributes would be more aligned with users' requirements. Hu and Liu sorted product attributes with the order of their occurrence counts, they counted and displayed the user numbers with different sentiment tendencies [Hu and Liu (2004a)]. Moreover, they provided some sentences extracted from reviews to help users obtain more detail on the product attributes, as shown in Fig. 2.4. Lu *et al.* predicted the ratings on product attributes by classification method, and extracted some representative phrases to enhance users' understanding on rating of every attribute [Lu *et al.* (2009)].

> *Digital_camera_1:*
>   Feature: **picture quality**
>   Positive: 253
>   <individual review sentences>
>   Negative: 6
>   <individual review sentences>
>   Feature: **size**
>   Positive: 134
>   <individual review sentences>
>   Negative: 10
>   <individual review sentences>
>   ...

Fig. 2.4   The example of sentiment summary on product attributes

Chapter 3

Preliminaries

In general, reviews are presented as vectors according to special feature presentation in the bag-of-words (BOW) framework. Based on this transformed form, different classification algorithms can be applied on opinion identification. To measure the effectiveness of opinion analysis, some common evaluation metrics are presented. This chapter introduces some preliminaries on above contents for opinion analysis.

3.1 Review presentations for opinion analysis

More and more users prefer to write reviews on various social network platforms to share their opinions. These user-generated contents are valuable for many Web applications, such as business and government intelligence, recommendation system. It is necessary to identify the user opinions automatically. Opinion analysis, also called opinion mining and opinion analysis, targets at identifying the user opinion (or sentiment) orientations expressed in reviews. Formally, it can be defined as following:

Definition 3.1 (Opinion analysis). Given a review set $R = \{r_1, r_2, \ldots, r_n\}$ and an opinion label set $L = \{l_1, l_2, \ldots, l_n\}$, opinion analysis function I assigns each review r_i with an opinion label:

$$\hat{l}_{r_i} = I(r_i) \tag{3.1}$$

where $1 \leq i \leq n, \hat{l}_{r_i} \in L$.

The volume of online reviews is very large, and it is updated very quickly. Opinion analysis on reviews manually is time-consuming and error-prone. Machine learning is one of the effective ways to identify the reviewers' opinions automatically. The BOW framework is usually used to present reviews, by which reviews are transformed into vectors. As shown in Fig. 3.1, each review is denoted

27

as a *m*-dimensional vector and every component of vector is the corresponding value of a feature.

$$
\begin{array}{c}
\quad\quad\quad\quad\quad \textbf{Feature 1}\ \textbf{Feature 2}\ \cdots\ \textbf{Feature m} \\
\begin{array}{c}
\textbf{Review 1} \\
\textbf{Review 2} \\
\vdots \\
\textbf{Review n}
\end{array}
\left[
\begin{array}{cccc}
V_{1,1} & V_{1,2} & \cdots & V_{1,m} \\
V_{2,1} & V_{2,2} & \cdots & V_{2,m} \\
\vdots & \cdots & \cdots & \vdots \\
V_{n,1} & V_{n,2} & \cdots & V_{n,m}
\end{array}
\right]
\end{array}
$$

Fig. 3.1   A diagram of review vectorization in BOW framework

To achieve this transformation, two base factors, feature template and feature function must be determined in advance. The former means what type of feature would be used to present reviews, such as *unigram* and *bigram*. The latter maps each feature in the review vector to a value, which could be *frequency*, *presence*, *TF-IDF*, and so on.

Feature templates can be divided into *general type* and *special type*. The features of *general type* refer to ones like *unigram* and *bigram*, whose values would be calculated by the predetermined feature functions. The features of *special type* are determined by analyzing the current tasks, such as the count of adjectives in review and the length of review. Some typical feature selection methods [Yang and Pedersen (1997)] used in traditional text classification would also be adapted for opinion analysis tasks, which are described as follows:

(1) *frequency threshold.* The term with a frequency in reviews over a special threshold is treated as a feature. A basic assumption is that the terms with low frequency cannot provide useful information for opinion analysis, and they would not have an impact on analysis effectiveness. Based on such assumption, the *frequency threshold* can reduce the dimension of feature space. At the same time, if the terms with low frequency happen to be the noise, it would improve classification accuracy. The *frequency threshold* is the simplest technique for feature selection, but the above assumption is not always true for opinion analysis tasks. For example, a term with strong sentiment, which is an obscure word, would be omitted in such case.

(2) *information gain.* This method evaluates the terms' information quantity for classification [Lewis and Ringuette (1994)]. Larger a term's information quantity is, more important it is. Given a class set $C = \{C_1, C_2, \ldots, C_n\}$, the information gain of term t is defined as:

$$G(t) = -\sum_{i=1}^{k} P(C_i) \log P(C_i) + P(t) \sum_{i=1}^{k} P(C_i|t) \log P(C_i|t)$$

$$+ P(\bar{t}) \sum_{i=1}^{k} P(C_i|\bar{t}) \log P(C_i|\bar{t}) \tag{3.2}$$

where $P(X)$ denotes the probability of X.

(3) *mutual information.* The mutual information can be used to measure the ties between term and class, by which terms would be determined whether to be features, as done in Refs. [Schütze *et al.* (1995); Wiener *et al.* (1995)]. For example, when to classify whether a review is *positive* or *negative*, the relationship of term t with two sentiment labels are calculated as following:

$$I(t,l) = \log \frac{P(t,l)}{P(t) \times P(l)}$$

$$\approx \log \frac{A \times N}{(A+C) \times (A+B)} \tag{3.3}$$

where l is the *positive* label or *negative* label, A is the number of times term t and label l co-occur, B is the number of times term t occurs without label l, C is the number of samples with label l but not include term t, and N is the total number of reviews. At last, the average or maximum value of *mutual information* with different labels can serve as the term t's score:

$$\begin{cases} I_{avg}(t) = P(l_{positive})I(t,l_{positive}) + P(l_{negative})I(t,l_{negative}) \\ I_{max}(t) = \max\{I(t,l_{positive}), I(t,l_{negative})\} \end{cases} \tag{3.4}$$

(4) χ^2 *statistic.* For classification tasks, this method considers the independence between term t and label l [Yang and Pedersen (1997)]. If term t is independent of any label, it would be not useful to classify reviews. For the example in (3), the χ^2 *statistic* value of term t and label l is computed as follows:

$$\chi^2(t,l) = \frac{N \times (AD - CB)^2}{(A+C) \times (B+D) \times (A+B) \times (C+D)} \tag{3.5}$$

where A is the number of times t and l co-occur, B is the number of times the t occurs without l, C is the number of times l occurs without t, D is the number of times neither l nor t occurs, and N is the total number of reviews. The term t's score can be determined with average or maximum value of χ^2 *statistic*, which is similar to that in *mutual information*.

(5) *term strength*. The term t's importance is quantified by its frequency occurring in closely related documents in Ref. [Yang (1995)]. Let d_i and d_j to be a pair of related documents, the *term strength* of term t is defined as

$$S(t) = P(t \in d_i | t \in d_j) \qquad (3.6)$$

where the related documents refer to those belong to the same cluster after clustering processing.

For these five feature selection methods above, *information gain, mutual information*, and χ^2 *statistic* require the class information of documents. Yang and Pedersen compared them for document classification based on k Nearest Neighbor (kNN) and Linear Least Squarest Fit (LLSF) in Ref. [Yang and Pedersen (1997)]. They found that χ^2 *statistic* and *information gain* are the most effective in their experiments, which was similar to *frequency threshold*. The *term strength* took the second place, and the *mutual information* was the worst one.

The N-gram is the most commonly used *general type* feature in opinion analysis, such as *unigram* and *bigram*. Pang *et al.* compared eight feature presentation methods including *unigram*, *bigram*, the combination of them with feature frequency or presence in review polarity classification implemented by Naive-Bayes, maximum entropy and Support Vector Machine (SVM) respectively in Ref. [Pang *et al.* (2002)]. The SVM with information of feature presence based on *unigram* outperformed the others in their experiments, whose accuracy was 82.9%. On the basis of unigram and bigram, the features were expanded with frequent word sub-sequences and dependency sub-tree in Ref. [Matsumoto *et al.* (2005)], which improved the opinion identification performance.

As presented above, frequency and presence are used generally in sentiment classification [Matsumoto *et al.* (2005); Pang *et al.* (2002)]. The classic *tfidf* schema was compared with its variants for opinion analysis in Ref. [Paltoglou and Thelwall (2010)]. The authors emphasized that expressing sample vectors with emotional information via supervised methods was helpful for predicting sentiment polarity. Moreover, features can be weighted with some external resources, such as WordNet[Miller *et al.* (1990)]. But it does not always perform better in this way, since the sentiment of word is domain-aware. In Ref. [Martineau *et al.* (2009)], a new feature weighting function called Δ*tfidf* was proposed for sentiment polarity classification, by which the importance of discriminative terms could be identified and boosted. In Ref. [Lin *et al.* (2012b)], mutual information was applied to identify term's sentiment polarity and evaluate its contribution by term frequency, by which we achieved a good classification performance. For the methods in Refs. [Martineau *et al.* (2009)] and [Lin *et al.* (2012b)], term sentiment information was integrated into the feature value to improve the opinion analysis accuracy, which will be discussed in detail in Chapter 4.

3.2 Single classifier methods

Opinion analysis can be treated as a classification problem. The supervised learning methods try to find a classification function C, which assigns each review r transform into a feature vector X with a class label y. The classifier is trained on a finite labeled sample set $\{(r_i, y_i)|i = 1, ..., N\}$, and the object is to minimize the expected error, i.e.,

$$C^* = \underset{C \in H}{argmin} \sum_{i=1}^{N} loss(C(X_{r_i}, y_i)) \tag{3.7}$$

where *loss* is a predefined loss function and H is a set of classification functions called the hypothesis. In sentiment classification, the vector X_{r_i} is the vectorization result of r_i. The label y stands for the sentiment class. In this book, we focus on sentiment polarity classification, which means to detect whether a review is positive or negative.

(1) Naive Bayes Classification

Naive Bayes Classification assumes that all features are independent, whose classification rule is as following:

$$f(X) = \underset{Y=\{C_h, C_l\}}{argmax} (P(Y) \prod_{j:x_j=1} P(x_j = 1|Y)) \tag{3.8}$$

where x_j is the component of review vector X, $P(Y)$ and $P(x_j|Y)$ are the probability calculated based on the training samples. Unfortunately, the independence assumption of features does not always exist in many real-word situations.

(2) Decision Tree

The decision tree classification model is a direct tree for classifying instances, in which the internal nodes denote features or attributes, the leaf nodes denotes classes [Li (2012)]. For a classification task, it tests the feature of an instance from the root node firstly. Secondly, it assigns instance with child node according to the testing result. Then the feature on current node is tested. The process is repeated until the instance is assigned with a leaf node, by which the class of instance is determined.

The essence of decision tree's learning process is to induce a set of classification rules, which often involves three steps: feature selection, decision tree construction and pruning. The typical learning algorithms include ID3 [Quinlan (1986)], C4.5 [Quinlan (1993)], and CART [Olshen and Stone (1984)]. The decision tree is easy to understand and implement, and it can handle large-scale reviews. But its classification error rate will improved quickly when the count of classes is increased.

(3) **Maximum Entropy Model**

The maximum entropy principle deems that the model with maximum entropy is the best one among all probability models. The maximum entropy classification determines the class l of a review r with the following exponential form [Pang *et al.* (2002)]:

$$P(l|r) = \frac{1}{Z} \exp(\sum_i \lambda_{i,l} F_{i,l}(r,l)) \tag{3.9}$$

where Z is a normalization function, $\lambda_{i,l}$ is the feature-weight parameter, large $\lambda_{i,l}$ means that feature i is considered to be a strong indicator for class l, and $F_{i,l}$ is a *feature/class function* for feature i and class l, which is defined as follows:

$$F_{i,l}(r,l') = \begin{cases} 1 & n_i(r) > 0 \wedge l' = l \\ 0 & otherwise \end{cases} \tag{3.10}$$

where $n_i(r)$ is the number of feature i occurs in review r. Importantly, the *maximum entropy model* makes no assumptions about the relationships between features, so it might potentially perform better when conditional independence assumptions are not true.

(4) **Support Vector Machine**

SVM [Cortes and Vapnik (1995)] maps the points non-separable in low dimension space into the high dimension space, which makes them separable. Unlike the Naive Bayes classification and maximum entropy model, SVM tries to find the large margin to separate the samples belonging to different classes. In the binary classification tasks, the basic idea behind the training procedure is to find a hyperplane that not only separates the review vectors in one class from the others, but also for which the margin is as large as possible.

To simplify feature analysis in later section, the evaluation is restricted to *linear* SVM in this book, which learns a weight vector $\hat{\omega}$ and bias term b, such that a review X_j can be classified by:

$$\hat{l} = sign(\hat{\omega} \cdot X_j + \hat{b}). \tag{3.11}$$

Theoretically, SVM can achieve the global optimal solutions. Its decision function is determined by few support vectors, and the computational complexity depends on the count of such vectors. Therefore, SVM has relatively strong generalized ability based on few training samples.

3.3 Evaluation metrics

To measure the effectiveness of opinion analysis, the first thing is to collect ground truth. One main challenge encountered by opinion analysis is the acquisition of ground truth, since opinions expression is a strong subjective problem. For the same review, different users may consider that it express different opinions. Especially for the case of multiple opinion classes, the situation gets worse. Thus, most opinion analysis research focus on two extreme classes: *positive* and *negative*, such as Refs. [Pang *et al.* (2002); Turney (2002); Hatzivassiloglou and McKeown (1997); Venkatasubramanian *et al.* (2011); Matsumoto *et al.* (2005); Dave *et al.* (2003); Gamon (2004); Mullen and Collier (2004); Lin *et al.* (2012c,a)] .

To obtain the gold data for verifying the effectiveness of opinion analysis, the following two ways are commonly applied:

(1) Manual labeling

Labeling samples one by one manually is too inefficient to produce enough labeled samples for training. Thus, semi-automatic methods based on few manual labeled samples might be feasible. Intuitively, it is easy for human to distinguish the positive reviews from the negative ones. Based on some words with strong sentiments, it might suffice to simply produce a list of such words and rely on them alone to predict the polarity of review.

Unfortunately, Pang *et al.* showed that the classification effectiveness of this method was poor in Ref. [Pang *et al.* (2002)]. They asked two graduate students to choose good indicator words for positive and negative sentiments in movie reviews independently. Their selections and the labeling accuracy based on counting the number of the proposed words are shown in Table 3.1. The authors pointed out that the brevity of the human-produced lists was a factor in the relatively poor performance results.

On the other side, different understanding on the same word or sentence for different people would make the things get worse, because the text comprehension is influenced by the readers' cultural background, education, experience, and so on. Therefore, Manual labeling reviews is a time-consuming and error-prone process. Some more effective ways need to be sought to gather the gold data.

Table 3.1   Semi-automatic label methods based on manually-labeled words [Pang *et al.* (2002)]

	Proposed word lists	Accuracy
Human 1	positive: dazzling, brilliant, phenomenal, excellent, fantastic negative: suck, terrible, awful, unwatchable, hideous	58%
Human 2	positive: gripping, mesmerizing, riveting, spectacular, cool, awesome,thrilling, badass, excellent, moving, exciting negative: bad, cliched, sucks, boring, stupid, slow	64%

(2) Labeling automatically based on the rating of review

Fortunately, most online review sites provide the function of user rating, which can summary user's opinions in his/her review on the corresponding object. For example, Amazon has a five star rate system, and IMDB has a ten score rate system, as shown in Fig. 3.2. This information can be used to label review as *positive* or *negative*. Blitzer *et al.* regarded Amazon reviews with four or five stars as positive reviews, and those with one or two stars as negative reviews in Ref. [Blitzer *et al.* (2007)]. Mullen and Collier treated the average rate as the boundary between positive reviews and negative reviews in Ref. [Mullen and Collier (2004)].

☆☆☆☆☆ **iPhone 5S**, October 23, 2013

By **Majed K. Alghurabi** (Riyadh, Saudi Arabia) - See all my reviews
REAL NAME

Amazon Verified Purchase (What's this?)

I liked the device and the new Touch ID feature. I didn't find any difference between iPhone 5 & 5S in regards of the Camera! I don't think that the iPhone 5 owners will find it attractive to upgrade from their phones to 5S!

(a) A review from Amazon

Typical action mixed with a cheesy and illogical script
☆☆☆☆☆☆
Author: ThePterodactylGynecologi from United States
27 July 2013

*** This review may contain spoilers ***

The Wolverine is OK at best, even with Hugh Jackman's usual superb acting. Most of the tell from the situation who is gonna die and who is gonna hit who several seconds before scenes, but these scenes are scattered very far apart.

(b) A review from IMDB

Fig. 3.2   Two review examples

The second way seems to be more reliable than the first one, since the ratings

Table 3.2　A 2×2 Contingence Table

Review number	Actual positive	Actual negative
Predict positive	a	b
Predict negative	c	d

are given by reviewers when they write the reviews.

Based on the ground truth, no matter how they are collected, various evaluation metrics can be used to measure the effectiveness of opinion analysis. The most commonly used index is the accuracy, which is defined as following.

$$accuracy = \frac{a+d}{a+b+c+d} \qquad (3.12)$$

where a, b, c and d are described in Table 3.2.

The further investigations can be taken for positive reviews and negative reviews respectively by precision, recall and F-measure, which are calculated as follows.

$$precision = \frac{tp}{tp+fp} \qquad (3.13)$$

$$recall = \frac{tp}{tp+fn} \qquad (3.14)$$

$$F_\beta = (1+\beta^2)\frac{precision \cdot recall}{(\beta^2 \cdot precision) + recall} \qquad (3.15)$$

Notably, Equations 3.13–3.15 focus on either *positive* or *negative*. For an instance, if the *positive* review plays a more important role in an application, then the tp is the count of positive reviews predicted as *positive*, the fp is the count of negative reviews predicted as *positive*, and the fn is the the count of positive reviews predicted as *negative*.

However, these three metrics do not seem to provide anything better than simple *accuracy*. In the domain of sentiment classification for reviews, it is often acceptable to sacrifice *recall* for *accuracy* [Tang *et al.* (2009)]. The customers always are not interested in all reviews on a product, they would focus on some of them. From this perspective, the *accuracy* is more important than *recall*.

The correlation is a standard measure of the degree to which two variables are linearly related, which is defined as

$$CorrCoefficient = \frac{S_{PA}}{S_P \cdot S_A} \qquad (3.16)$$

where

$$S_{PA} = \frac{\Sigma_i(p_i - \bar{p}) \cdot (a_i - \bar{a})}{n-1}$$

$$S_P = \frac{\Sigma_i(p_i - \bar{p})^2}{n - 1}$$

$$S_A = \frac{\Sigma_i(a_i - \bar{a})^2}{n - 1}$$

and p_i is the estimated value for instance i, a_i is the actual value for instance i, $\bar{x}$ is the average of x, and n is the total number of instances. The scale of correlation coefficient is $[0,1]$, large value means good linear relation between these two variables. Mishne and Rijke used the *correlation coefficient* to evaluate how much degree the fluctuation patterns of sentiment are predicted by the classification model [Mishne and de Rijke (2006)]. Moreover, they also applied *relative error* on measuring the main difference between the predicted values and the true ones:

$$RelError = \frac{\Sigma_i(p_i - a_i)}{\Sigma_i(a_i - \bar{a})} \tag{3.17}$$

Wei and Gulla [Wei and Gulla (2010)] use One-error Loss (L_O) function, the Symmetric Loss (L_S) function and the Hierarchical Loss (L_H) function to measure classification performance on their constructed sentiment ontology tree. These three loss function are defined as follows.

$$\begin{cases} L_O(\hat{y}, l) = \mathfrak{B}(\exists i : \hat{y}_i \neq l_i) \\ L_S(\hat{y}, l) = \Sigma_i \mathfrak{B}(\hat{y}_i \neq l_i) \\ L_H(\hat{y}, l) = \Sigma_i \mathfrak{B}(\hat{y}_i \neq l_i \wedge \forall j \in \mathscr{A}(i), \hat{y}_j = l_j) \end{cases} \tag{3.18}$$

where $\hat{y}$ is the prediction label vector and l is the true label vector, the Boolean function $\mathfrak{B}(S)$ is 1 if and only if the statement S is true, $\mathscr{A}(i)$ denotes a set of nodes that are ancestors of node i in the sentiment ontology tree.

3.4 Potential datasets

Many opinion analysis tasks are conducted for online reviews [Pang *et al.* (2002); Wei and Gulla (2010); Dave *et al.* (2003); Blitzer *et al.* (2007); Pang and Lee (2004); Turney (2002); Mullen and Collier (2004); Pan *et al.* (2010); Wu *et al.* (2010c); Tan and Cheng (2009)], since reviews contain rich opinion of users. Amazon[1] is a good potential data source because it has abundant types of goods and large volume reviews. These reviews can be achieved by the Amazon's application program interface.

Liu of the UIC (University of Illinois at Chicago) released a review dataset[2] crawled from Amazon, which contains four main product reviews: books, music,

---

[1]www.amazon.com

[2]https://www.cs.uic.edu/~liub/FBS/sentiment-analysis.html

DVD and manufactured products like computer, electronics, and so on. Table 3.3 shows some statistical information on this dataset.

Table 3.3 Some statistic information on Liu's dataset

Category	Reviews	Reviewed Products	Reviewers
books	2493087	637120	1076746
DVD	1327456	221432	503884
music	633678	60292	250693
manufactured products	228422	36692	165608
other	1155389	239597	149117
all	5838032	1195133	2146048

Each review contains eight fields: *product ID, Reviewer ID, Rating, Date, Review Title, Review Body, Number of Helpful Feedbacks*, and *Number of Feedbacks*. Moreover, this dataset also provides some useful information such as product name, price, product description, and Amazon user's profile like user ID, user name, review number and user's personal statement, and so on.

Another Amazon dataset[3] was released by Blitzer of University of Pennsylvania in August 2007. The data is stored in XML (eXtensible Markup Language) format. Each review includes *review ID, product ID, product name, product type, helpful feedbacks, rate, review title, posted time, reviewer name, reviewer location* and *review body*. Every type of reviews contains labeled samples and unlabeled samples, where the reviews with four or five stars are marked as *positive* reviews and those with one or two star(s) as *negative* ones. Notably, not all types of labeled product reviews are balance in this dataset. For example, the labeled reviews on office supplies are made up of 64 *negative* reviews and 367 *positive* reviews, but book reviews contains 1,000 positive, 1,000 negative and 973,194 unlabeled reviews. Some statistic information on this dataset is showed in Table 3.4.

Table 3.4 Some statistic information on Blitzer's Amazon dataset

Category	Reviews	*Positive* reviews	*Negative* reviews	Unlabeled reviews
25	1422530	21972	16576	1383982

Pang of Cornell University released a movie review set[4] in 2004, which

---

[3]http://www.cs.jhu.edu/~mdredze/datasets/sentiment/. The dataset is updated in March 2009
[4]http://www.cs.cornell.edu/people/pabo/movie-review-data

contains movie reviews extracted from IMDB[5]. In order to avoid reviewer bias, only twenty reviews per author are kept, resulting in a total of 320 authors. These reviews are labeled by a binary classifier based on user's rates, and they consist of 1,000 *positive* reviews and 1,000 *negative* ones. The classifier determines the polarities of reviews based on some well-defined rules.

Mass *et al.* of Stanford University released a larger IMDB review set[6], which is made up of 25,000 *positive* reviews, 25,000 *negative* reviews and 50,000 unlabeled ones. They treated reviews with seven points or more in IMDB rating system as the *positive* ones, and those with four or less as the *negative* ones. At the same time, the URL (Uniform Resource Locator) of each review was also provided for users.

Many e-Commerce websites would be the potential data sources, such as Amazon, eBay[7], TripAdvisor[8], Epinions[9], resellerratings[10] and taobao[11]. Table 3.5 shows some available information on these data sources.

Table 3.5   Some available information on potential review sources

	Amazon	eBay	TripAdvisor	Epinions	IMDB	ResellerRatings	Taobao
Average rate	√	√	√	√	√	√	√
Rate distribution	√	√	√	√	√	√	√
Recommended review	√	√	—	√	√	—	√
Review title	√	√	√	√	√	—	—
Review body	√	√	√	√	√	√	√
Review rate	√	√	√	√	√	√	—
Posted time	√	√	√	√	√	√	√
Helpful feedbacks	√	√	√	—	√	—	√
Reviewer profile	√	√	√	√	√	√	√
Comment on review	√	—	—	√	—	√	—
Rate on aspects	—	√	√	√	—	√	√

---

[5]http://www.imdb.com
[6]http://www.andrew-maas.net/data/sentiment
[7]http://www.ebay.com
[8]http://www.tripadvisor.com
[9]http://www.epinions.com/
[10]http://www.resellerratings.com/
[11]http://www.taobao.com. Taobao is the biggest e-Commerce website in China.

Chapter 4

Terms' sentiment-based review opinion analysis

This chapter will analyze the relationships of terms with sentiment labels based on information theory, and propose a method by applying information theoretic approach on sentiment classification of documents. Mutual information is adopted to quantify the sentiment polarities of terms in a review. Then the terms are weighted in vector space based on both sentiment scores and contribution to the document. Extensive experiments are performed on the sets of multiple product reviews, and experimental results show that the proposed approach is more effective than these traditional ones.

4.1 Introduction

When reviews are transformed into vectors by traditional feature presentations, the terms' sentiment information is ignored. However, the opinion orientation of review has a close relationship with the terms sentiment. This is one of the primary causes that traditional feature presentations work poorly in opinion analysis. Pang *et al.* introduced machine learning methods to opinion analysis on document granularity in Ref. [Pang *et al.* (2002)]. They compared multiple feature presentations with different classification algorithms, and pointed out that the combination of *unigram*, *presence* and SVM achieved the best effectiveness. But their methods do still not take the term sentiment information into account. If such sentiment information is integrated into the values of features, the effectiveness of opinion analysis should be improved, which is verified by our experiment discussed in Section 4.4.

The general sentiment dictionary is a simple and direct way to capture term sentiment. SentiWordNet is such a dictionary, which was developed by Esuli and Sebastiani of the University di Padoval [Esuli and Sebastiani (2006b)]. The main limitation of applying general sentiment dictionaries on capturing words' sentiment is that many words' sentiment is domain-depended or topic-sensitive. Namely, a word can express various sentiment in different domains. For example, the word "predictable" is a good attribute of electronics, but it expresses negative sentiment for reviewing a novel or movie. On the other hand, some words' meaning must be determined with the context, such as "aggressive".

As presented in Chapter 3, the χ^2 *statistic* (shown in Equation 3.5) achieves rather good performance for traditional text classification tasks. But Example 4.1 shows that the χ^2 *statistic* is not suitable for the sentiment polarity classification, since the χ^2 values of any term with two labels are equal. Then, the term's sentiment cannot be distinguished. Therefore, the χ^2 *statistic* cannot capture the sentiment information of terms.

Example 4.1. For sentiment polarity classification, when the sentiment labels l_1 and l_2 are given, the χ^2 values of term t and each label can be calculated as follows:

$$\chi^2(t,l_1) = \frac{N \times (A_{l_1}D_{l_1} - C_{l_1}B_{l_1})^2}{(A_{l_1} + C_{l_1}) \times (B_{l_1} + D_{l_1}) \times (A_{l_1} + B_{l_1}) \times (C_{l_1} + D_l)}$$

$$\chi^2(t,l_2) = \frac{N \times (A_{l_2}D_{l_2} - C_{l_2}B_{l_2})^2}{(A_{l_2} + C_{l_2}) \times (B_{l_2} + D_{l_2}) \times (A_{l_2} + B_{l_2}) \times (C_{l_2} + D_2)}$$

According to the definitions of these parameters, $\chi^2(t,l_1)$ is equal to $\chi^2(t,l_2)$, since $A_{l_1} = B_{l_2}, B_{l_1} = A_{l_2}, C_{l_1} = D_{l_2}, D_{l_1} = C_{l_2}$.

To integrate the term's sentiment information into feature value, Martineau *et al.* proposed a feature function called *Delta TF-IDF* (Δ *TF-IDF* for short) in Ref. [Martineau *et al.* (2009)], which used the count of positive reviews and negative reviews containing term t to evaluate its sentiment orientation. The weight value of term t in review r can be calculated by the following formula:

$$V_{t,d} = C_{t,d} \times \log_2 \left(\frac{P_t}{N_t} \right) \tag{4.1}$$

where $C_{t,d}$ is the number of term t occurs in document d, N_t is the number of negative training samples containing term t, and P_t is the number of positive training samples containing term t. The part of *log* in Equation 4.1 evaluates the sentiment of term t for review r, which expresses positive sentiment with positive number and negative sentiment with negative number.

Equation 4.1 evaluates term's sentiment according to the number of different polarity reviews including the term. It means that terms would express the sentiment class of the reviews including the term more times. However, for a term in reviews, if the number of positive reviews is the same to that of the negative ones, this term could not prefer to express the sentiment class.

Example 4.2. Given 10 positive reviews and 10 negative ones. There are 9 positive reviews containing term t, and t occurs k ($k \geq 2$) times in each of them. At the same time, term t occurs in 9 negative review one time respectively. Intuitively, term t should express the positive sentiment. But its sentiment score is $\log_2 \frac{9}{9} = 0$ according to the Equation 4.1.

This is because $\Delta TF\text{-}IDF$ does not consider the distribution of term in reviews, which leads to the inexact sentiment identification of term. Therefore, a more effective way is required to capture the term's sentiment information. In this chapter, a new feature function is presented. Firstly, term's information is captured by supervised learning methods. Then, such information is integrated with term's contribution to determine the term's value. The effect of this feature function is verified in latter experiments.

4.2 Capturing the terms' sentiment information

Given a training set $S = \{\langle s_1, l_{s_1} \rangle, \ldots, \langle s_n, l_{s_n} \rangle\}$, where s_i denotes the ith training sample and l_{s_i} the polarity label of s_i, and a set of testing samples $U=\{u_1, \ldots, u_r\}$ without labels. Our task is to predict the polarity labels of all testing samples. In this subsection, we present how to apply mutual information into capturing a term's sentiment polarity.

In probability theory and information theory, the mutual information can capture the difference between the joint distribution on (X, Y) and the marginal distributions on X and Y. It is a quantity that measures the mutual dependence of two random variables. Formally, the mutual information of two discrete values is evaluated as follow:

$$MI(x,y) = \log_2 \frac{P(x,y)}{P(x)P(y)} \tag{4.2}$$

where $P(x,y)$ is the joint probability of x and y, $P(x)$ and $P(y)$ are the marginal probability of x and that of y respectively.

Now a term's relationships with each label are quantified by mutual information. Given N labeled samples, A is the number of times term t and label l co-occur, B is the number of times term t occurs without label l, C is the number of samples with label l but not include term t. Thus the mutual information $MI(t,l)$ of t and l can be evaluated by:

$$MI(t,l) = \log_2 \frac{P(t,l)}{P(t)p(l)} \approx \log_2 \frac{A \times N}{(A+B) \times (A+C)} \tag{4.3}$$

This book focuses on two types of labels: the positive label l_p and the negative label l_n. It is clear that the term t in Example 4.2 is more relative with the positive label according to Example 4.4. It means term t would prefer to express positive sentiment. Therefore, the mutual information is more suitable for capturing the sentiment information of terms in review set.

Example 4.3. For Example 4.2, the mutual information of term t and the positive label is

$$MI(t,l_p) = \log_2 \frac{9k \times 20}{(9k+9) \times (9k+1)}$$

$$= \log_2 \frac{20k}{(k+1) \times (9k+1)}$$

The mutual information of term t and the negative label is

$$MI(t,l_n) = \log_2 \frac{9 \times 20}{(9+9k) \times (9+1)}$$

$$= \log_2 \frac{2}{k+1}$$

Since $k \geq 2$, $MI(t,l_p) > MI(t,l_n)$ holds.

In general, if term t is positive, the value of $MI(t,l_p)$ is relatively high and $MI(t,l_n)$ is relatively low according to the Equation (4.3). Thus, the sentiment score $S_{MI}(t,l_p)$ of term t on l_p can be derived from a linear combination of $MI(t,l_p)$ and $MI(t,l_n)$, the $S_{MI}(t,l_n)$ is similar to $S_{MI}(t,l_p)$:

$$\begin{cases} S_{MI}(t,l_p) = \alpha MI(t,l_p) + (1-\alpha)(-MI(t,l_n)) \\ S_{MI}(t,l_n) = \alpha MI(t,l_n) + (1-\alpha)(-MI(t,l_p)) \end{cases} \tag{4.4}$$

where $0 \leq \alpha \leq 1$ and it is a weighting parameter which reflects the contributions of $MI(t,l_p)$ and $MI(t,l_n)$.

To measure the goodness of term t in a global feature presentation, we integrate $S_{MI}(t,l_p)$ and $S_{MI}(t,l_n)$ into one sentiment score $S_{MI}(t)$ with Equation (4.5):

$$S_{MI}(t) = \begin{cases} |S_{MI}(t,l_p)| & \text{if } S_{MI}(t,l_p) > S_{MI}(t,l_n) \\ 0 & \text{if } S_{MI}(t,l_p) = S_{MI}(t,l_n) \\ -|S_{MI}(t,l_n)| & \text{if } S_{MI}(t,l_p) < S_{MI}(t,l_n) \end{cases} \tag{4.5}$$

If $S_{MI}(t,l_p) > S_{MI}(t,l_n)$ holds, term t tends to express positive sentiment in current domain and overall sentiment score of t, $S_{MI}(t)$, is set to a positive value. On the contrary, if term t tends to negative sentiment, its $S_{MI}(t)$ value should be negative.

To achieve an intuitive understanding, Table 4.1 shows the top 15 positive unigrams and negative ones for reviews on kitchen appliances and books in our real-world dataset respectively. We can observe that most of these terms reflect correct sentiment inclinations intuitively. Here, the term "not_waste" denotes a tag "not_" is appended to the term "waste", which will be described in Section 4.4. When someone does not like something, he or she can often say "Don't waste your time on ...". Thus, we should properly process the negatory words. Some outliers like "Lodge" and "Trotsky" and so on will also be discussed further in Section 4.4.

Table 4.1 The top 15 positive unigrams and negative ones in reviews on kitchen appliances and books ($\alpha = 0.7$)

Kitchen appliances		Books	
Positive	Negative	Positive	Negative
awesome	not waste	nationalism	disappointing
loves	defective	Trotsky	weak
amazing	refund	masterpiece	flat
quiet	probe	awesome	predictable
favorite	returned	favorites	poorly
ease	junk	investigation	repetitive
impressed	worst	imagination	not waste
Lodge	not unit	explores	stupid
collection	dangerous	rare	barely
remember	failed	Crichton	useless
sizes	not recommend	vivid	unrealistic
durable	followed	illustrated	boring
cleans	ring	copies	endless
excellent	told	Vietnam	zero
Dutch	candy	sons	pathetic

4.3 Identifying review's sentiment polarity

This subsection will present how to identify the sentiment polarities of reviews automatically. To evaluate the contribution of term t to review r, the frequency of t in r is integrated with the sentiment score $S_{MI}(t)$. Thus the weight $V(t,r)$ for term t in review r is defined as:

$$V(t,d) = tf_{t,r} \times S_{MI}(t) \tag{4.6}$$

where the $tf_{t,r}$ is the frequency of term t in review r.

Some researches like Ref. [Pang *et al.* (2002)] reported that the presence feature was comparable and even better than the frequency feature due to the sparsity of opinionated words. But our key observation in pre-experiment was that this would depend on the analyzed domains, and even it could achieve the worst performance sometimes. Thus the frequency of terms is applied on capturing their contribution to the review in this book.

The procedure of sentiment polarity classification using mutual information is described in Algorithm 4.1. Firstly, for each term t in the training set, its sentiment score S_{MI} value is evaluated with Equations 4.3–4.5. Secondly, the $V(t, r_i)$ value of each term t in each training sample r_i is determined with Equation 4.6. Let symbol $X = (\mathbf{x}_1, \ldots, \mathbf{x}_n)$ denotes the training set using the proposed approach, where $\mathbf{x}_i$ is the vector of the ith review. And the vector $\mathbf{x}_i$'s component $x_{i_{t,r_i}}$ refers to the $V(t, r_i)$ of term t and training sample r_i. $Y = (\mathbf{y}_1, \ldots, \mathbf{y}_n)$ is similar to X, excepting $\mathbf{y}_j$ denotes the vector of testing sample. Then, a classifier C is generated by training on the set X and is used to generate the set $L = \{l_1, \ldots, l_n\}$ of sentiment polarity labels of testing samples.

Algorithm 4.1 Sentiment Polarity Classification based on *MI*

Input: the training set $S = \{\langle r_1, l_{r_1} \rangle, \ldots, \langle r_n, l_{r_n} \rangle\}$
    the testing set $U = \{u_1, \ldots, u_t\}$
Output: predicted labels set $L = \{\hat{l}_{u_1}, \ldots, \hat{l}_{u_t}\}$
1: $L = \varnothing, S' = \varnothing$;
2: **for each** term t generated by the reviews in S **do**
3:     Calculating $S_{MI}(t, l_p)$ and $S_{MI}(t, l_n)$ with the Equation 4.4;
4:     Calculating the sentiment score $S_{MI}(t)$ of term t with the Equation 4.5;
5: **end for**
6: **for** $i = 1$ **to** n **do**
7:     Transforming training sample r_i into vector $\mathbf{x}_i$ with Equation 4.6;
8:     $S' = S' \cup \{(\mathbf{x}_i, l_{r_i})\}$;
9: **end for**
10: Training the C on S';
11: **for** $i = 1$ **to** t **do**
12:     Transforming testing sample u_i into vector $\mathbf{y}_i$ with Equation 4.6;
13:     $L = L \cup \{C(\mathbf{y}_i)\}$;   //Using the classifier C to predict the label of $\mathbf{y}_i$
14: **end for**
15: **return** L;

4.4   Experiments

We will show a series of experiments on opinion analysis for different types of product reviews from a real-world dataset to verify the effectiveness of the proposed method in this section.

4.4.1 *Experiment setting*

A real-world dataset[1] reorganized by Blitzer *et al.* [Blitzer *et al.* (2007)] is prepared for our experiments, which consists of reviews of books (**B** for short), DVDs (**D**), electronics (**E**) and kitchen appliances (**K**) from Amazon[2]. The reviews marked with 4 or 5 stars are attached with a positive label, and those with 1 or 2 stars are attached with a negative label. Each product domain contains 1,000 positive and 1,000 negative reviews. Five-fold cross validation is applied in our experiments. All tests are implemented by LIBSVM[3] with a linear kernel function, the rest parameters remain the default values.

The data set is preprocessed according to the following steps:

(1) All punctuations are removed but the stop words are retained.
(2) All unigrams with length less than 3 are omitted. No stemming or lemmatizing is used because they are detrimental to classification accuracy [Leopold and Kindermann (2002)].
(3) Like the preprocesses done in Ref. [Pang *et al.* (2002)], the negatory words from reviews are omitted and the tag "not_" is appended to the words following the negatory word in a sentence. For instance, the sentence "It doesn't work smoothly" would be altered to become "It not_work not_smoothly".

Two types of features used commonly in sentiment classification are focused: *unigram* and *bigram*. For each one, the proposed approach is compared with other weighting methods including *frequency*, *presence* and *ΔTF-IDF* respectively:

(1) *TF*senti*: SentiWordNet 3.0 is used to determine the sentiment score of a term, the term is weighted by the product of its frequency and its sentiment score.
(2) *frequency*: The term frequency is regarded as its weight.
(3) *presence*: Considering whether the term occurs in a document.
(4) *ΔTF-IDF*: Described in Section 4.1.
(5) *TF*MI* (the proposed method): Weighting terms with Equation 4.6.

The accuracy is applied on evaluating the effectiveness of proposed approach in our experiments, which is defined as Equation 3.12 presented in Section 3.3.

---

[1] http://www.cs.jhu.edu/~mdredze/datasets/sentiment/
[2] http://www.amazon.com
[3] http://www.csie.ntu.edu.tw/~cjlin/libsvm/

4.4.2   Results and discussion

The first experiment concerns the effectiveness of the sentiment score S_{MI} presented in Section 4.2. Recalling the results in Table 4.1, almost all of the top 15 sentiment scores of positive unigrams and negative ones in reviews of books and kitchen appliances reflect strong sentiment direction correctly. Now we focus on the analysis of some outliers. The "Lodge" in column 1 of Table 4.1 always expresses the neutral sentiment without context. But the "Lodge" is a famous manufacture, whose products on kitchen appliances including Dutch ovens retrain a lot of popular credibility. There are 10 reviews total on the products of Lodge in our dataset, and 90% of them are positive. That is why the term "Lodge" builds stronger relationship with positive label. Seven of the ten reviews on sharpeners are labeled as positive, and the left three negative. Thus, the term "sharpeners" is more closely related to the positive label. The terms "probe" and "candy" are similar to this case, the former is included in 15 negative reviews and 1 positive review, and the later occurs in 6 negative reviews and in 1 positive review. In our dataset, the Dutch ovens have received wide praise, but "ovens" does not occur in Table 4.1 because "oven" is used by reviewers sometimes and no stemming processes are applied in our experiments. We omit such discussion on DVDs and electronics domains, which are similar to the cases discussed above.

For the results in Table 4.1 in book domain, "Trotsky" and "Crichton" are two writers, whose books have gained recognition in our dataset. The most reviews on books referring to the term "Vietnam" are positive (five positive reviews and only one negative review), the term "sons" is similar to it. For the term "zero" in books, the negative reviews contain some negative information including "zero information" and "zero interesting anecdotes", while "zero" is often regarded as the neutral one considered in isolation. Thus, our approach captures term's sentiment orientation correctly.

The *unigram* is one of the most commonly used feature type in text classification. The second experiment concerns the effectiveness of *TF*MI* based on *unigram*. Figure 4.1 shows the results of accuracy comparisons on four product domains. Our approach, *TF*MI*, achieves the best performance in all product domains. On the one hand, both *Delta tfidf* and *TF*MI* outperform the other three weighting methods invariably. On the other side, *TF*MI* is better than *Delta TF-IDF* in all domains, especially the accuracy of *TF*MI* is about 2.4% higher than that of *delta TF-IDF* in **D**. Thus, both *TF*MI* and *Delta TF-IDF* are effective ways for unigram to sentiment classification and the second half, $log_2 \frac{N_t}{P_t}$, of Equation 4.1 can also capture the sentiment polarities of terms effectively, but our approach is more effective. At the same time, *tf*senti* performs poorly in total, because a word often expresses several meanings. When it is considered solely, it is difficult to determine its sentiment polarity in a review. The feature *presence* is not always superior to the feature frequency, that is true in **D** and **K** but false in **B** and **E**. Comparatively, it seems the feature *frequency* is better than feature *presence* based on the average accuracy in all domains.

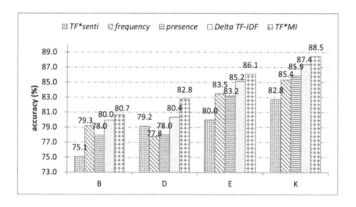

Fig. 4.1   Accuracy comparisons based on unigram

Figure 4.2 shows the comparisons among the weighting methods based on *bigram*. Like the previous experiment on *unigram*, our approach, *TF*MI*, achieves the best performance in all domains, and the accuracy is improved more significantly compared with the results in Fig. 4.1. It is worth noting that *Delta TF-IDF* is worse than the frequency and presence in electronics domain for the *bigram*, and that the *Delta TF-IDF* is not very stable in some sense. Comparatively, the proposed approach always achieves the best performance in all domains.

Furthermore, Fig. 4.1 and 4.2 show that the classification accuracies on reviews of electronics and kitchen appliances are higher than those in books and DVDs domains clearly. The sentiment expressions on books or DVDs are often more subtle than those of general products. For instance, a review of a book is written as following: "When I read this book, I can't conceal my rage on the leading man, his ugly personality make me sick." The terms "rage", "ugly", and "sick" always express intensive negative emotion, while we concern them without context. But the reviewer is praising this book indeed.

At last, the impact of varying the parameter α based on *unigram* and *bigram* is investigated respectively. Recalling the discussion in Subsection 4.2, term t's score of polarity label l is linear combination of two parts: t's mutual information with l and that with the opposite of l. As shown in Figs. 4.3 and 4.4, when *TF*MI*

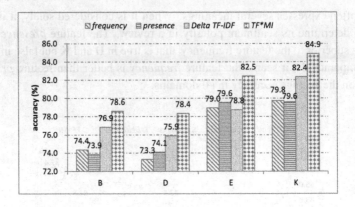

Fig. 4.2   Accuracy comparisons based on bigram

achieves the best accuracy, the value of α always locates at [0.5, 1]. Thus, the relation between t and l seems to be more importance than that between t and the opposite of l, which is consistent with our intuitive. For unigram, the value of α should range from 0.5 to 0.8, and from 0.8 to 1 for bigram. Notably, whatever the value of α set is, accuracy of our approach is higher than that of *Delta TF-IDF* in almost all cases as long as $\alpha \geq 0.5$ holds.

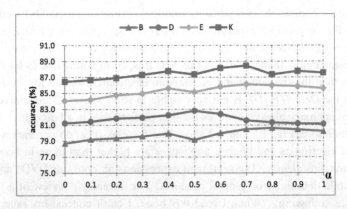

Fig. 4.3   Accuracies of *TF*MI* based on *unigram* under varying value of α

4.5   Summary

The traditional feature presentations do not consider term's sentiment information during the process of review vectorization, which makes the classification

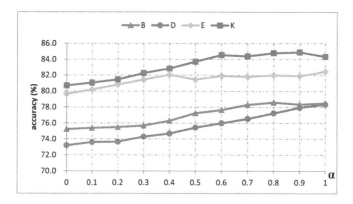

Fig. 4.4   Accuracies of *TF*MI* based on *bigram* under varying value of α

effectiveness inadequate for opinion analysis tasks. This chapter presents a new feature function, which integrates term's sentiment information with its contribution to review. Firstly, the mutual information is used to evaluate the terms sentiment score. Secondly, the term's contribution to review is quantified by term's frequency. Based on these two factors, a new feature function is formed for opinion analysis. Such method can not only achieve good classification effectiveness, but also capture the sentiment of *n-gram* ($n > 1$), which is not available for general sentiment dictionaries. At last, a series of experiments on opinion analysis are conducted for multiple domains on a real-world dataset to verify the effectiveness of the proposed method. The results show that the proposed method achieves the best performance compared with the traditional feature functions.

Chapter 5

Multiple classifier system for opinion analysis

More and more classifiers are available for user to perform an opinion analysis task. However, it is troublesome for them to choose the best one for their tasks, since each classifier always achieves different performance for different domains. On the other hand, how to improve the effectiveness based on these available classifiers is an interesting question. To deal with such problems, a three phase framework is developed based on assembling multiple classifiers. In order to choose the optimal combination of classifiers, a criterion is proposed for estimating the quality of the combination. Moreover, the effectiveness of the number of classifiers selected is also studied experimentally. Extensive experiments are performed to demonstrate the effectiveness of our solution.

5.1 The limitation of single classifier methods

To construct an effect classifier for opinion analysis tasks, users are need to determine three basic factors of classifier: feature type, feature function and classifier algorithm. There are many options for these three factors. As discussed in previous chapter, the common used feature types include *unigram*, *bigram*, and so on, the feature functions include *frequency*, *presence*, Δ *TF-IDF* and *TF*MI* etc., classification algorithms like NaiveBayes, maximum entropy (MaxEnt for short) and SVM are always applied on opinion analysis. The combinations of these options would construct lots of classifiers. Unfortunately, none of these classifiers can always perform optimally in all domains because of its inherent properties. Thus, it is difficult for users to predetermine which classifier should be applied due to lots of alternatives, especially for those who are not familiar with the analyzed domains. Besides, how to further improve the classification effectiveness for opinion analysis tasks based on so many available classifiers is an interesting and meaningful problem.

In order to give an intuitive understanding on the difficulty of classifier selection, Table 5.1 shows the classification accuracies by using three classification algorithms based on *unigram* for four domains[1]. The key observation is that the best classifier is various for different domains. For example, the combination of MaxEnt and Δ*TF-IDF* are the optimal for the DVD and Kitchen appliances, MaxEnt and *TF*MI* is the best combination for Electronics, NaiveBayes and *presence* are the best option for Books. Notably, Table 5.1 considers only the *unigram*. If other feature types such as *bigram* are treated as options, the problem of user's choice on classifier will become more complicated.

Table 5.1   Comparisons on opinion classification accuracies for different domains based on *unigram*

Classification algorithm	Feature function	Domain			
		Books	DVDs	Electronics	Kitchen appliances
MaxEnt	*frequency*	79.1	79.2	82.6	84.6
	presence	79.8	81.0	83.9	85.5
	Δ*TF-IDF*	80.9	**82.5**	84.8	**88.4**
	*TF*MI*	80.7	81.7	**85.2**	88.1
NaiveBayes	*frequency*	80.7	79.6	83.1	86.0
	presence	**81.3**	80.1	84.9	87.4
	Δ*TF-IDF*	78.4	76.5	79.8	84.1
	*TF*MI*	77.9	76.1	79.7	84.3
SVM	*frequency*	78.5	78.5	81.9	84.0
	presence	77.0	78.0	81.8	85.3
	Δ*TF-IDF*	78.5	79.6	82.8	86.6
	*TF*MI*	79.4	81.9	83.8	87.6

This chapter proposes a three phase ensemble learning framework to deal with the problem of being difficult to select classifier for users. The following two problems are discussed further:

(1) Given a set of candidate classifiers, how to select an optimal set of classifiers to achieve the best performance?
(2) For the set of classifiers chosen, how to ensemble them?

[1] The results listed in Table 5.1 are generated by the classifiers, which are trained with part of labeled samples. The rest of labeled samples will be used to train the ensemble classifier (more detail would be discussed in Section 5.4). However, the classifiers in experiments of Chapter 4 are trained with all labeled samples. Therefore, the accuracies in Table 5.1 are slight different with those in Chapter 4.

5.2 The ensemble framework

For simple presentation, some symbols are defined at first. Given a feature type set $F = \{f_1, \ldots, f_u\}$, a feature function set $W = \{w_1, \ldots, w_m\}$, and a classification algorithm set $C = \{c_1, \ldots, c_n\}$. The $\mathbf{x}_{r,j}$ denotes the sample vector constructed by the feature type f_r and the feature function w_j, $C_{(k,r,j)}$ denotes the constructed classifier using classification algorithm c_k trained on training vectors with the form of $\mathbf{x}_{(r,j)}$. Thus, the triples $\Phi = (k, r, j)$ indicates a classifier uniquely. Let $com_{(C_{\Phi_1}, \ldots, C_{\Phi_M})}$ be a combination of M base classifiers, $\Phi_i \in \{(k, r, j)|k = 1 \ldots n, r = 1 \ldots u, j = 1 \cdots m\}$. Our target is to find the prior combination of classifiers for the classification tasks:

$$com^* = \underset{com \in COM_{all}}{argmin} \sum_{i=1}^{N} loss(\Gamma(com_{(C_{\Phi_1}, \ldots, C_{\Phi_M})}(r_i, y_i))), \qquad (5.1)$$

where COM_{all} is the set of all possible combinations with M classifiers, Γ is a fusion function which maps the M predicted results of sample r_i generated by M base classifiers to an ultimate label.

To figure out the problem of classifier selection difficulty, a three phase multiple classifier ensemble learning framework is proposed, as shown in Fig. 5.1. The proposed framework contains three phases: the training phase of conceptual classifiers, the evaluation phase of the classifier set and the ensemble learning phase.

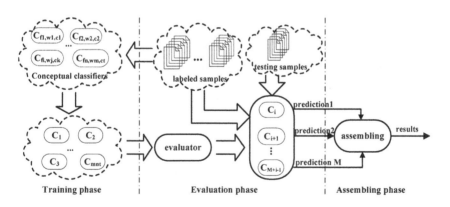

Fig. 5.1   The three phase ensemble learning framework for opinion analysis

A conceptual classifier $C_{fi,wj,ck}$ is made up of the three basic factor, which are selected from the feature type set F, feature function set W and classification algorithm set C respectively. In the proposed framework, all available conceptual classifiers are trained with the label samples to generate optional classifiers.

Secondly, the optimal set of base classifiers is chosen from these candidates. The results predicted by the set of base classifiers are treated as new labeled samples for training an assembling classifier.

The prediction process of unlabeled samples is similar to that of the training assembling classifier. Firstly, the base classifiers predict the label of a sample. Then these predictions serve as the input of an assembling classifier, and the sample's label is generated.

5.3   Evaluating the quality of classifier combination

Given u feature types, m feature functions, and n classification methods, umn classifiers can be constructed. If k classifiers are chosen, there will be C_{umn}^K possible options. It is a thorny problem for users to make a choice without an effective evaluating criterion.

It is clear that classification accuracy is one of the most important index of classifier performance. Thus, the average accuracy of base classifiers should be treated as an essential part of the evaluating criterion. Assuming that two classification hyperplanes of classifier C_1 and C_2 are shown as Fig. 5.2. Both of these two classifiers cannot classify all of the samples correctly. An useful information is that classifier C_1 can classify some samples correctly which are misclassified by classifier C_2, and some samples misclassified by C_1 can be classified correctly by classifier C_1. Therefore, it is possible for us to boost these complementary information to correct some misclassified predictions. Intuitively, the error predictions are those inconsistences by two classifiers. This is to say that those samples locate in the dashed area of Fig. 5.2. Thus, the diversity of prediction of base classifiers should be another important factor for evaluating the quality of classifier set. Moreover, if the classifiers, which make the same predictions, are assembled, the final accuracy is impossible to be higher than that of any one of base classifiers.

As discussed above, for the selection of base classifiers, those with large diversity of predictions should be preferred based on their average accuracy. The Fleiss' kappa [Fleiss *et al.* (2013)] is a statistical measure for assessing the agreement among several classifiers when assigning labels to a number of samples. Let N be the total number of samples, k the number of classifiers, and n the number of labels. The $n_{i,j}$ refers to the number of classifiers which assign sample S_i to the label y_j. Then the kappa value, κ, is defined as following:

$$\kappa = \frac{p_o - p_e}{1 - p_e}, \qquad (5.2)$$

where p_o is the overall proportion of observed agreement, p_e is the overall

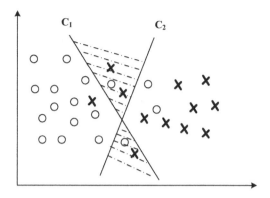

Fig. 5.2   Classification hyperplanes of two classifiers

proportion of chance-excepted agreement:

$$p_o = \frac{1}{Nk(k-1)} \left(\sum_{i=1}^{N} \sum_{j=1}^{n} n_{ij}^2 - Nk \right)$$

$$p_e = \frac{1}{(Nk)^2} \sum_{j=1}^{n} \left(\sum_{i=1}^{N} n_{ij} \right)^2$$

According to the Equation 5.2, the greater value the κ is, the classifiers will have higher agreement. If the classifiers are in full agreement, then $\kappa = 1$. If there is no agreement among the classifiers, then $\kappa = 0$. The consistency of predictions can be measured by different values of κ, as shown in Table 5.2[2]. Since the disagreement is required in the evaluating criterion, $1 - \kappa$ is used to measure the diversity of predictions.

As discussed earlier, the combination of base classifiers with great average accuracy and diversity is a good choice. But if the accuracy can implicate the diversity, namely, accuracy improvement leads to diversity increase inevitably, or the increase of diversity must lead to accuracy increase, only one of them is enough for measuring the quality of classifier set. But Example 5.1 shows there is nothing deterministic about accuracy improvement leading to higher diversity, namely, higher $1 - \kappa$. Likewise, there is nothing deterministic about the reducing of average accuracy leading to lower diversity. Therefore, both of them should be included into our estimation criterion at the same time.

Example 5.1. Assuming three classifiers (C_1, C_2, C_3) assign 10 samples $(S_1, ..., S_{10})$ with 2 labels (0, 1) independently, the predictions are shown in Table 2. The true labels of samples are shown in the last row of Table 5.3. The

---

[2]https://en.wikipedia.org/wiki/Fleiss%27_kappa

Table 5.2 The relationship between the value of κ and agreement

κ	Interpretation
< 0	Poor agreement
0.01–0.20	Slight agreement
0.21–0.40	Fair agreement
0.41–0.60	Moderate agreement
0.61–0.80	Substantial agreement
0.81–1.00	Almost perfect agreement

accuracy of C_1 is 80%, C_2 70% and C_3 80%, then the average accuracy is 76.67% and the $1 - \kappa$ is about 0.34 according to the Equations (5.3)–(5.5). We make some modifications in Table 5.3: $C_2(S_6) = 1$, $C_2(S_8) = 0$ and $C_3(S_7) = 1$. Now the average accuracy increases to 80%, but the $1 - \kappa$ decreases to 0.33.

Table 5.3 The predictions of three classifiers

	S1	S2	S3	S4	S5	S6	S7	S8	S9	S10
C1	0	0	1	1	0	1	1	1	1	1
C2	1	0	0	0	0	0	0	1	1	1
C3	0	0	0	0	0	0	0	1	1	1
true label	0	0	0	0	0	1	1	1	1	1

Formally, the quality of a set of base classifiers could be evaluated based on the accuracy and the diversity as follows.

$$Q_{com(C_{\Phi_1},...,C_{\Phi_M})} = \alpha \frac{\sum_{i=1}^{M} accuracy(C_{\Phi_i})}{M} + (1 - \alpha)\left(1 - \kappa_{com(C_{\Phi_1},...,C_{\Phi_M})}\right) \quad (5.3)$$

where $accuracy(C_{\Phi_i})$ is the accuracy of base classifier C_{Φ_i} ($1 \leq i \leq M$), $\kappa_{com(C_{\Phi_1},...,C_{\Phi_M})}$ is the Fleiss' kappa value of base classifier set, α ($0 \leqslant \alpha \leqslant 1$) is used to weight the average accuracy and diversity. Notably, α should be assigned a relatively great value, since the accuracy is more important, which will be discussed further in Section 5.5.

5.4 Assembling a set of base classifiers

The optimal combination of base classifiers can be chosen according to the Equation 5.3. These base classifiers are used to predict the label of a sample, and there will be multiple predictions. Then, a fusion function Γ is devised to generate the ultimate label of the sample based on these predictions.

For assembling the base classifiers, an ensemble algorithm for multiple classifiers based on *stacking* [Džeroski and Ženko (2004); Zenko *et al.* (2001)] is proposed. As shown in Algorithm 5.1, the algorithm contains base-level training phase and meta-level training phase. In the base-level training phase, the training set is divided into two disjoint subset with unequal sizes (without loss of generality, let $|Part_1| > |Part_2|$) (Line 1). In order to make the base classifier achieve strong generalization ability, the $Part_1$ is applied on training the base classifiers (Line 4). The $Part_2$ serves as the testing sample set, which is predicted by base classifiers (Line 6). All of predictions made by base classifiers are integrated with the true labels of samples to form a new training samples for the next training phase (Line 10), which will generate $|Part_2|$ new training samples. These new samples are applied on training an ensemble classifier C_{meat} (Line 12). Moreover, to improve the generalization ability of base classifiers, k-fold cross validation process can be carried out on the original training set to construct more meta-level training samples.

Algorithm 5.1 Assembling multiple classifiers based on *stacking* (ACS)

Input: the chosen base classifier set S,
       the labeled sample set T
Output: the ensemble classifier C_{meta}
  1: Dividing T into two disjoint subsets $Part_1 Part_2$ ($|Part_1| > |Part_2|$);
  2: $T_{meta} = \varnothing$;
  3: **for** $i = 1$ TO $|S|$ **do**
  4:     Using $Part_1$ to train the base classifier C_i in S;
  5:     **for** $j = 1$ TO $|Part_2|$ **do**
  6:         Using C_i to predict the label $\hat{l}_{C_i}^j$ of s_j in $Part_2$;
  7:     **end for**
  8: **end for**
  9: **for** $k = 1$ TO $|P_2|$ **do**
 10:     $T_{meta} = T_{meta} \cup \{(\hat{l}_{C_1}^k, \hat{l}_{C_2}^k, \ldots, \hat{l}_{C_{|S|}}^k, l_k)\}$;
 11: **end for**
 12: Using new sample in T_{meta} to train the ensemble classifier C_{meta};
 13: **return** C_{meta};

For an unlabeled testing sample, base classifiers produce M predictions, whose predictions are treated as the input of ensemble classifier C_{meta}, and the generated result serves as the label of the testing sample. Notably, only a part of labeled samples can be used to train the base classifiers, since the Algorithm *ACS* needs some samples to train the ensemble classifier. However, all labeled samples can be used to train the classifier for the traditional single classifier methods. Thus, the generalization ability of base classifier is slight worse than that of classifier in traditional single classifier methods, but this loss of performance will be compensated by the meta-level training phase.

5.5   Experiments

In this section, a series of experiments on opinion analysis are conducted on a real-world dataset to verify the effectiveness of the proposed method in multiple domains.

5.5.1   *Experiment setting*

The dataset used in this chapter is the same as that in Chapter 4, which includes the reviews from Amazon on books (B), DVD (D), electronics (E) and kitchen appliances (K). Three feature types are focused on: *unigram*, *bigram* and the mixture of them. The feature functions include *frequency*, *presence*, Δ *TF-IDF*, and *TF-MI* presented in previous chapter. Classification algorithms include NaiveBayes[3], MaxEnt and SVM[4]. For simplicity, ΔTF-*IDF* and *TF-MI* are based on *unigram*. Therefore, there are 24 candidate base classifiers. The MaxEnt is treated as the meta-level classification algorithm[5].

The preprocess of reviews is the same as that in previous chapter. The *accuracy* is used to evaluate the effectiveness of different methods, which is defined as Equation 3.12 presented in Section 3.3. The highest accuracy of single classifier among 24 candidate base classifiers for different domains serves as the baseline. The process of 4-fold cross validation is performed to generate meta-level training samples, but 5-fold cross validation is used to verify the final classification

---

[3]Implemented by WEKA. Available at http://www.weka.net.nz

[4]Implemented by LIBSVM with a linear kernel function. Available at http://www.csie.ntu.edu.tw/~cjlin/libsvm/

[5]The NaiveByes and SVM are treated as meta-classifier independently in our experiments, but their performances are poorer than the *stacking* with maximum entropy in our dataset.

accuracy. Unless otherwise noted, the number of base classifier is 5. And the parameter α in Equation 5.3 is set to 0.8.

5.5.2 Results and discussion

The first experiment focuses on the classification effectiveness of proposed method (*Q_ACS*), which chooses the optimal base classifier set based on the Equation 5.3 firstly and then uses the *ACS* (Algorithm 5.1) to assemble base classifiers. The *avg_single* refers to the average accuracy of 24 candidate base classifiers. The *best_single* is the highest accuracy of classifier among all of the candidates. For example, the classifier constructed by *unigram*, *ΔTF-IDF*, and MaxEnt achieves the highest classification accuracy (88.4%) for kitchen appliance domain, as shown in Table 5.1.

Figure 5.3 shows the effectiveness comparisons of opinion classifications for different domains. The thing to be noticed is that the results in Table 5.1 are only based on *unigram*. Thus, the highest accuracy for each domain is not always the accuracy of *best_single*. For instance, the highest accuracy of single classifier for book domain is achieved by the classifier constructed by Naive-Bayes based on *frequency*, the mixture of *unigram* and *bigram*, but not the Naive-Bayes based on *presence* and *unigram* in Table 5.1, in which the accuracy is 81.3%. As shown in 5.3, the proposed *Q_ACS* improves the accuracies for all domains significantly compared with the *avg_single*. For example, the accuracy of *Q_ACS* increases 6.7% for book domain, 7.9% for DVD domain, 5.5% for electronics domain and 5.8% for kitchen appliance domain. Another observation is that the poorer the effect of single classifier is, the more increase on effect the *Q_ACS* makes. This is because, with the improvement of base classifier's accuracy, the improvement on diversity among the base classifiers is less and less, in other words, the predictions of base classifiers become more and more consistent. On the other side, *Q_ACS* works better than the *best_single*. This means that users are needed to determine the available feature types, feature functions, and classification algorithms in the propose framework for opinion. An optimal set of base classifiers would be chosen by the quality evaluation metric to assemble, which will achieve the better performance than the single classifier methods. Notably, when users perform opinion analysis tasks for a special domain, it is always difficult for them to choose the classifier with the best performance.

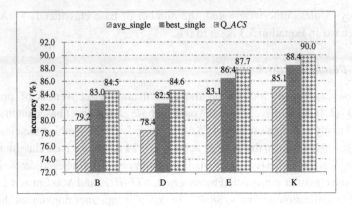

Fig. 5.3   The classification effectiveness for different domains

The quality of base classifier set is measured based on two factors: *accuracy* and *diversity*, whose weights are turned by the parameter α. As a result analysis above, the higher the value of α is, the more important the *accuracy* is. In contrast, the *diversity* is more important. The next experiment analyzes the α's impact on classification accuracies in different domains. As shown in Fig. 5.4, when the value of α locates in $[0.7, 0.9]$ for each domain, the highest accuracy is achieved. Consequently, the average accuracy of base classifiers plays a key role in our solution, and the diversity makes an indispensable complementarity, because the performance is decreased when the α is set to 0.9 or 1. Moreover, this experiment shows that the values of α are stable for different domains in our experiments, which makes the users easy to set the α, which is a good property.

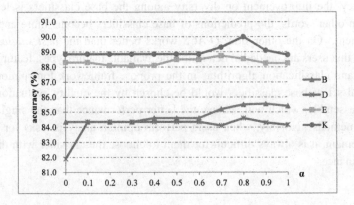

Fig. 5.4   The α's impact on classification accuracies

The third experiment focus on the effectiveness of the selection criterion. As discussed as before, there are 24 base classifiers, and five of them are chosen as a combination, then there are 42,504 possible combinations. The estimation value Q for each combination is calculated with Equation 5.3, and these values are sorted by descending order. Six combinations of base classifiers are picked out in turn, which locate at the 1st, 8500th, 17000th, 25500th, 34000th, and 42504th location of the sorted results respectively. These six points divide the sorted results into five approximative equal parts. Figure 5.5 shows that the accuracies are descending with the declining of the combination quality. Consequently, our selection criterion is effective for capturing the combination quality of base classifiers.

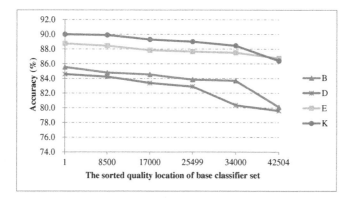

Fig. 5.5   The effect of selection criterion on base classifiers

The last experiment considers the problem of how many base classifiers should be used in our framework. The number of base classifiers are set to 3, 4, 5, 6, and 7 respectively, and their classification accuracies for each domain are compared. The effects of different base classifier numbers are shown in Fig. 5.6. A key observation is that the number of base classifiers does not affect the performance too much, which means that the accuracy difference between two cases in each domain is less than 1% in our dataset. Therefore, the number of base classifier is easy to determine, which is another good property of our solution.

5.6   Summary

In general, it is always difficult for users to choose the best classifier for opinion classification for a special domain, especially for those who are not familiar with the analyzed domain. Moreover, how to improve the classification accuracy based

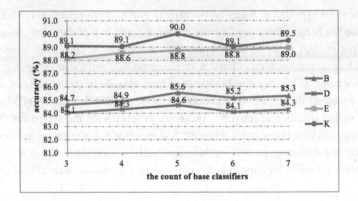

Fig. 5.6   Varying the total number of base classifiers

on available classifiers is a problem which is worth to explore.

This chapter proposes a three phase ensemble learning framework for opinion analysis. In this framework, users only need to determine the available feature types, feature functions and classification algorithms. An optimal set of base classifiers is chosen automatically based on the proposed quality evaluating metric, which is based on average accuracy and diversity of classifiers. In addition, the number of base classifiers does not affect the performance of our solution too much, which is verified experimentally. At last, a series of experiments are carried out for different domains on a real-world dataset to demonstrate the effectiveness of our solution.

Chapter 6

Optimization of base classifier selection

In previous chapter, a three phase framework is proposed for opinion analysis, in which users only need to determine the available basic factors of classifier, and an optimal set of classifiers would be selected based on their accuracies and diversity to assemble automatically. The classification effect of the proposed solution is always better than that of the best single classifier. Unfortunately, this solution encounters the Combinatorial Explosion Problem of classifier set selection, which limits its availability for the case of large number of candidate base classifiers. Therefore, we design an approximate algorithm to select the optimal classifier set, which can be proven to be 2-approximation.

6.1 The necessity of selection optimizing on base classifiers

When the machine learning methods are applied to opinion analysis, a conceptual classifier is constructed by three base factors: feature type, feature function and classification algorithm. This conceptual classifier is trained with label samples to generate a classifier entity (classifier for short). But there will be lots of conceptual classifiers, since the available factors are so many. And the classifier with optimal performance is various for different domains. Thus, it is always difficult for users to determine which classifier should be used for their opinion analysis tasks. Further, how to improve the accuracy based on these available classifier is a valuable research issue.

As discussed in previous chapter, the method of multiple classifier ensemble is an effective way to handle such problem. In Refs. [Lin *et al.* (2012c)], [Li and Zong (2008)] and [Xia *et al.* (2011)], the base classifiers were trained based on the predetermined feature types, feature functions, and classification algorithms. And then, the predictions were integrated to generate the final prediction by different integrating strategies. But how to choose the base classifiers was not explored in these work. In previous chapter, a three phase framework was proposed for opinion analysis, in which user only needed to determine the available basic factors of classifier, and an optimal set of classifiers would be selected according to a proposed quality evaluating metric based on their accuracies and diversity. At last, an algorithm was devised to assemble the chosen classifiers. This selection metric was verified by a series of experiments. Unfortunately, with the increases of base classifier count, the number of possible base classifier combinations would increase rapidly, which makes the search space too large to find the optimal base classifier combination. Therefore, we focus on handling the Combinatorial Explosion Problem of classifier set selection in this chapter.

6.2 Combination optimization

In the literatures on classification in machine learning domain, there are a lot of classifiers. And each of these classifiers has its own characteristic. None of them always achieves the best performance in all analyzed domains. However, the ensemble learning methods have stronger generalization capability than the single classifier methods. It is generally regarded that the base classifiers with strong generalization capability and diversity is the key point for ensemble learning algorithms [Krogh *et al.* (1995)].

It is not a good idea to employ the member classifiers as much as possible, because the diversity among them will decrease with the increasing number of member classifiers. Thus, an effective method need to be devised to select the optimal member classifier set and it needs more memory and more computation. In this chapter, the base classifiers are selected based on their accuracies and the diversity among them.

Supposing k member classifiers selected, the optimal classifier set $D = \{C_i | i = 1, ..., N\}$, and the accuracy of classifier C_i is denoted as $A(C_i)$. A distance function *dist* is applied on measuring the classification diversity between classifier C_i and C_j, which quantifies the difference between the two classification result sets generated by classifier C_i and C_j. Then, the member classifier selection problem can be formulated as the following optimization problem.

$$\max_{S \subseteq D, |S| = k} \Psi(S) \tag{6.1}$$

$$\Psi(S) = \lambda \sum_{C_i \in S} A(C_i) + (1 - \lambda) \sum_{C_i, C_j \in S} dist(C_i, C_j) \tag{6.2}$$

where S is the set of selected member classifiers, k is the number of base classifiers, and $\lambda (0 \leqslant \lambda \leqslant 1)$ is the weight parameter to adjust the contributions of accuracy and diversity.

When the count of base classifiers is increased, the combination count would be increased quickly, which makes finding the optimal solution of the objective function impossible. Therefore, a greedy algorithm is devised to find the approximate solution.

6.3 A greedy algorithm for base classifier selection

To quantify the diversity of base classifiers, the *disagreement measure* [Skalak (1996)] serves as the distance function[1], which evaluates the ratio between the number of samples on which one classifier is correct and the other is incorrect to the total number of samples, i.e.,

$$dist(C_i, C_j) = \frac{N_{01} + N_{10}}{N} \tag{6.3}$$

where N is the total number of predicted samples, N_{01} is the number of samples predicted incorrectly by classifier C_i but correctly by classifier C_j, N_{10} is the number of samples predicted correctly by classifier C_i but incorrectly by classifier C_j.

Assuming $S \cap G = \varnothing$ and $S, G \subseteq D$. The relative definitions on diversity of classifier sets are given as follows.

Definition 6.1 (The internal diversity of classifier set). For the classifier set S, the internal diversity is the sum of the diversity of pairwise classifiers in S, i.e.,

$$dist(S) = \sum_{C_i, C_j \in S} dist(C_i, C_j) \tag{6.4}$$

Definition 6.2 (The diversity of classifier sets). For the classifier sets S and G, their diversity are as follows

$$dist(S, G) = \sum_{C_i \in S, C_j \in G} dist(C_i, C_j) \tag{6.5}$$

For any subset S of D, classifier $C_u \in D - S$, let $dist_{C_u}(S) = \sum_{C_v \in S} dist(C_u, C_v)$ and $A_{C_u}(S) = A(C_u)$ to be gains on diversity and accuracy after adding the classifier C_u. This gain is denoted as $\Psi_{C_u}(S) = \lambda A_{C_u}(S) + (1 - \lambda)dist_{C_u}(S)$. According to the Equations 6.1 and 6.2 the proposed classifier selection Greedy Algorithm (*CSGA*) for selecting the base classifiers is shown as Algorithm 6.1.

---

[1] The distance function is different with that in previous, the main cause is that *disagreement measure* has some good properties, such as the triangle inequality, which will be proven in the following section

---

Algorithm 6.1 Classifier Selection Greedy Algorithm (*CSGA*)

Input: the optional classifier set D,
    member classifier number k,
    weight parameter λ
Output: member classifier set S

1: $S = \varnothing$;
2: **while** $|S| < k$ **do**
3:     Selecting the classifiers C_u from $D - S$, which maximizes the equation $\frac{\lambda}{2} A C_u(S) + (1 - \lambda) dist_{C_u}(S)$;
4:     $S = S \cup \{C_u\}$;
5:     $D = D - \{C_u\}$;
6: **end while**
7: **return** S;

6.3.1 *The theoretical analysis on* CSGA*'s approximation ratio*

In order to prove the algorithm *CSGA* to be 2-approximation, we introduce some definitions as follows.

Definition 6.3 (monotonicity). The function $f : 2^V \to \mathbb{R}$ is monotonous, if the inequality $f(A) \leqslant f(B)$ holds for any $A \subseteq B \subseteq V$.

Definition 6.4 (submodularity). The function $f : 2^V \to \mathbb{R}$ is submodular, if the inequality $f(A \cup \{e\}) - f(A) \geq f(B \cup \{e\}) - f(B)$ holds for any $A \subseteq B \subseteq V$ and $e \in V - B$.

The submodularity shows that the incremental gain of e decreases as the context in which e is considered grows from A to B. Recently, submodular functions have received attention in machine learning and information retrieval [Lin and Bilmes (2011); Kempe *et al.* (2003); Narasimhan and Bilmes (2007); Vee *et al.* (2008)], because such functions share a number of properties in common with convex and concave [Lovász (1983)].

Let $\Phi(S) = \lambda \sum_{C_i \in S} A(C_i)$, the following conclusion holds.

Theorem 6.1. *The function* $\Phi(S)$ *is monotonous and submodular.*

Proof. For any $T \subseteq G \subseteq S$, then $\Phi(T) = \lambda \sum_{C_i \in T} A(C_i)$ and $\Phi(G) = \lambda \sum_{C_i \in G} A(C_i)$.

Because $A(C_i)$ denotes the accuracy of classifier C_i, $A(C_i) \geq 0$ and $T \subseteq S$, We will get $\Phi(T) \leq \Phi(G)$.

Then, $\Phi(S)$ is monotonous according to the Definition 6.3.

For any $T \subseteq G \subseteq S, C_e \in S - G$, let $T' = T \cup \{C_e\}$ and $G' = G \cup \{C_e\}$ then

$$(f(T \cup \{C_e\}) - f(T)) - (f(G \cup \{C_e\}) - f(G))$$
$$= (\lambda \sum_{C_i \in T'} A(C_i) - \lambda \sum_{C_i \in T} A(C_i)) - (\lambda \sum_{C_i \in G'} A(C_i) - \lambda \sum_{C_i \in G} A(C_i))$$
$$= \lambda A(C_e) - \lambda A(C_e)$$
$$= 0.$$

Thus, $\Phi(S)$ is submodular according to the Definition 6.4. $\square$

Let A, B, and C denote three classifiers making binary classification on the sample set $S = \{s_1, s_2, \dots, s_N\}$, p_X^i is the prediction of sample s_i generated by classifier X, and $D_{X,Y} = \{s_i | p_X^i \neq p_Y^i\}$. Then, the following conclusion holds.

Theorem 6.2. *The distance function $dist(C_i, C_j)$ satisfies the triangle inequality.*

Proof. Assuming that there are x samples, for which classifier A and C make different predictions. Without loss of generality, supposing those samples are the first x samples in S, i.e., $D_{A,C} = \{s_1, \dots, s_x\}$.

Note that the $N_{01} + N_{10}$ is the number of different predictions generated by two classifiers. Then,

$$dist(A,C) = \frac{x}{N}$$

If $|D_{A,B}| = 1$, supposing the sample is s_i, then we only consider two cases: $s_i \in D_{A,C}$ and $s_i \notin D_{A,C}$.

For the case of $s_i \in D_{A,C}$, because we make binary classification in this work,

$$dist(A,B) + dist(B,C) = \frac{1}{N} + \frac{x-1}{N} = dist(A,C)$$

For the case of $s_i \notin D_{A,C}$,

$$dist(A,B) + dist(B,C) = \frac{1}{N} + \frac{x+1}{N} > dist(A,C)$$

If $|D_{A,B}| = k$ ($k > 1$), let y is the number of samples belong to $D_{A,C}$, for which A and B make different predictions, namely, the member number of the set $\{s_i | s_i \in D_{A,C} \wedge p_A^i \neq p_B^i\}$. Then,

$$dist(A,B) + dist(B,C)$$
$$= \frac{k}{N} + \frac{x-y+k-y}{N}$$
$$= \frac{x+2(k-y)}{N}$$

Since $k \geq y$ holds, the following inequality holds:

$$dist(A,B) + dist(B,C) \geq dist(A,C).$$

$\square$

Based on Theorem 6.2, the Lemma 6.1 can be get directly from Ref. [Ravi *et al.* (1994)].

Lemma 6.1. *Given two disjoint sets, namely G and S, the distance function dist, then the inequality* $(|G| - 1)dist(G,S) \geq |S|dist(G)$ *holds.*

Nextly, the algorithm *CSGA* will be proven to be 2-approximation based on the above theorems, lemma and the work in Ref. [Borodin *et al.* (2012)]. Assuming the set O is the optimal member classifier set, while S is the member classifier set generated by algorithm *CSGA*, S^i is the member classifier set generated in the ith iteration of *CSGA*.

Let $A = O \cup S^i$ and $C = O - A$, then A, B and C are pairwise disjoint. For ease of exposition, $\frac{1}{2}\sum_{C_i \in S} A(C_i)$ is denoted as $\Phi'(S)$. Next, the *CSGA* is started to prove to be 2-approximation as following.

Proof. When only one classifier is selected, the solution of *CSGA* is the exact optimal solution obviously.

If $|C| = 1$, then $i = k - 1$ and $S^i \subset O$. Let C_u is the selected classifier in next iteration. For any $C_v \in D - S$, the following inequality holds:

$$\frac{\lambda}{2}A_{C_u}(S^i) + (1-\lambda)dist_{C_u}(S^i) \geq \frac{\lambda}{2}A_{C_v}(S^i) + (1-\lambda)dist_{C_v}(S^i).$$

Then, after classifier C_u is selected,

$$\begin{aligned}
\Psi_{C_u}(S^i) &= \lambda A_{C_u}(S^i) + (1-\lambda)dist_{C_u}(S^i) \\
&\geq \frac{\lambda}{2}A_{C_u}(S^i) + (1-\lambda)dist_{C_u}(S^i) \\
&\geq \frac{\lambda}{2}A_{C_v}(S^i) + (1-\lambda)dist_{C_v}(S^i) \\
&\geq \frac{1}{2}\Psi_{C_v}(S^i).
\end{aligned}$$

Therefore, $\Psi(S) \geq \frac{1}{2}\Psi(O)$.

Now the case of $k > 1$ and $|C| > 1$ is analyzed. From the Lemma 1,

$$(|C| - 1)dist(B,C) \geq |B|dist(C)$$

$$\Rightarrow dist(B,C) \geq \frac{|B|}{|C|-1}dist(C) \tag{6.6}$$

$$(|C| - 1)dist(A,C) \geq |A|dist(C)$$

$$\Rightarrow \frac{|C| - |B|}{k}dist(A,C) \geq \frac{|A|(|C| - |B|)}{k(|C|-1)}dist(C) \tag{6.7}$$

$$(|A| - 1)dist(A,C) \geq |C|dist(A)$$

$$\Rightarrow \frac{i(|A| - 1)}{k(k-1)}dist(A,C) \geq \frac{i|C|}{k(k-1)}dist(A) \tag{6.8}$$

Because $O = A \cup C$ and $A \cap C = \varnothing$,

$$dist(A,C) + dist(A) + dist(C) = dist(O)$$

$$\Rightarrow \frac{i|C|}{k(k-1)}(dist(A,C) + dist(A) + dist(C)) = \frac{i|C|}{k(k-1)}dist(O). \quad (6.9)$$

Using $(6.6) + (6.7) + (6.8) + (6.9)$ together with $|A| = k - |C|$ and $|A| + |B| = i$, then

$$dist(A,C) + dist(B,C) - \frac{i|C|(p - |C|)}{k(k-1)(|C|-1)}dist(C) \geq \frac{i|C|}{k(k-1)}dist(O).$$

Since $k > |C|$ and $dist(A,C) + dist(B,C) = dist(S^i,C)$, then

$$dist(S^i,C) \geq \frac{i|C|}{k(k-1)}dist(O).$$

Like the proof on Theorem 6.1, the equation $\Phi'_{C_u}(S) = \frac{\lambda}{2}A_{C_u}(S)$ is proven to be monotonous and submodular. Then,

$$\sum_{C_v \in C} \Phi'_{C_v}(S^i) \geq \Phi'(C \cup S^i) - \Phi'(S^i) \geq \Phi'(O) - \Phi'(S),$$

and then

$$\sum_{C_v \in C} \Psi'_{C_v}(G^i) = \sum_{C_v \in C} (\phi'_{C_v}(S^i) + (1-\lambda)dist(C_v, S^i))$$

$$= \sum_{C_v \in C} \Phi'_{C_v}(S^i) + (1-\lambda)dist(C, S^i)$$

$$\geq (\Phi'(O) - \Phi'(S)) + \frac{(1-\lambda)i|C|}{k(k-1)}dist(O).$$

Let C_u is the classifier selected in the $(i+1)^{th}$ iteration, then

$$\Psi'_{C_u}(S^i) \geq \frac{1}{k}(\Phi'(O) - \Phi'(S)) + \frac{(1-\lambda)i}{k(k-1)}dist(O).$$

Consequently,

$$\Psi'_S = \sum_{i=0}^{k-1} \Psi'_{C_u}(S^i) \geq (\Phi'(O) - \Phi'(S)) + \frac{(1-\lambda)}{2}dist(O).$$

Therefore,

$$\Phi'(S) + (1-\lambda)dist(S) \geq (\Phi'(O) - \Phi'(S)) + \frac{(1-\lambda)}{2}dist(O)$$

$$\Leftrightarrow \frac{1}{2}\Phi'(S) + \frac{1-\lambda}{2}dist(S) \geq \frac{1}{2}\Phi'(O) - \frac{1}{2}\Phi'(S) + \frac{1-\lambda}{4}dist(O)$$

$$\Leftrightarrow \Phi'(S) + \frac{1-\lambda}{2}dist(S) \geq \frac{1}{2}\Phi'(O) + \frac{1-\lambda}{4}dist(O)$$

$$\Leftrightarrow \frac{1}{2}\Phi(S) + \frac{1-\lambda}{2}dist(S) \geq \frac{1}{4}\Phi(O) + \frac{1-\lambda}{4}dist(O)$$

$$\Leftrightarrow \frac{1}{2}(\Phi(S) + (1-\lambda)dist(S)) \geq \frac{1}{4}(\Phi(O) + (1-\lambda)dist(O))$$

$$\Leftrightarrow \Psi(S) \geq \frac{1}{2}\Psi(O).$$

$\square$

From the proof above, the algorithm *CSGA* is 2-approximation. In practice, the approximate solution generated by *CSGA* is very close to the optimal solution, which is verified in our experiments discussed in Section 6.4.

6.3.2   Time complexity analysis

Supposing that k classifiers are chosen from n optional ones, where n is much greater than k in general. If the exhaustion method is applied to search the optimal solution, all possible classifier combinations must be evaluated, and the time complexity is $O(n^k)$.

For the proposed algorithm *CSGA*, there are $n - i + 1$ ($1 \leq i \leq k$) comparisions in the procedure of selecting the ith member classifier. Then, the time complexity of *CSGA* is $O(n)$. This shows *CSGA* time complexity is linear, which makes the *CSGA* available in reality.

6.4   Experiments

In this section, a series of experiments are carried out for different domain reviews on real-world datasets to verify the effectiveness of the proposed methods.

6.4.1   Experiment setting

To verify the performance of the proposed methods, we carry out our experiments on six types of reviews: Apparels (**A**), Book (**B**), DVD (**D**), Electronics (**E**), Health appliance (**H**) and Sport-outdoor appliance (**S**). The preprocess of reviews is the same as those in previous chapters.

As discussed above, a classifier is constructed by three base facts: feature type, feature function and classification algorithm. In the following experiments, the applied feature types include *unigram*, *bigram* and the mixture of *unigram* and *bigram*. Four feature functions are considered in our experiments: frequency, present or not, $\Delta tfidf$ and $tf * MI$. For $\Delta tfidf$ and $tf * MI$, only the unigram is considered for simplicity. The classification algorithms of base classifiers contain the NaiveByes[2], maximum entropy (MaxEnt, for short) and SVM[3]. Then, there

---

[2]Implemented by WEKA. Available at http://www.weka.net.nz
[3]Implemented by LIBSVM with a linear kernel function. Available at http://www.csie.ntu.edu. tw/~cjlin/libsvm/

are 24 optional member classifiers. The MaxEnt classifier is used as meta-level classifier, namely the ensemble classifier.[4]

Nine different methods are compared with each other in the experiment. The 4-fold cross validation procedure is used on the labeled sample set to construct the meta-level training set, and 5-fold cross validation is used to estimate the overall classification performance. The compared methods are shown as follows.

(1) *avg_single*. The average accuracy of all optional classifiers.
(2) *best_single*. The highest accuracy among all optional classifiers.
(3) *bagging_DT*. The bagging technology with the decision tree.[5] The feature template and the feature function are the best among all the candidates. The iteration time is the best one no more than 70.
(4) *adaboost_DT*. The adaboost technology with the decision tree. The feature template, the feature function and the iteration times are determined with the same methods of the *adaboost*. The iteration time is the best one no more than 70.
(5) *random_forest*. An ensemble learning method for classification that operates by constructing a multitude of decision trees at training time and integrating the predictions by majority vote.
(6) *ramdom_ACS*. Selecting a set of member classifiers randomly and assembling them with the proposed algorithm *ACS*. We run this method ten times and average the classification accuracy.
(7) *CSGA_voting*. Selecting a set of member classifiers with the proposed algorithm *CSGA* and assembling with majority voting.
(8) *prune_eigcons*. The state art of technology proposed in Ref. [Xu *et al.* (2012)], which is used for ensemble pruning.
(9) *CSGA_ACS*. Selecting a set of member classifiers with *CSGA* and assembling with *ACS*.

6.4.2 *Results and discussion*

The ensemble learning are applied into solving the difficult problem on classifier selection faced by users. The algorithm *CSGA* is proposed to select a set of base classifiers firstly. Then the predictions of member classifiers are assembled by the algorithm *ACS*. The first experiment focuses on the accuracy of the proposed method. The experimental results are shown in Fig. 6.1. Since training classifier

---

[4]We also use NaiveByes and SVM as meta-classifier independently, but their performances are poorer than the *stacking* with maximum entropy in our datasets.

[5]The decision tree is compared with NaiveBayes in this context, the latter is slightly worse. It is similar to the adaboost.

is time-consuming, the default number of base classifier is set to 5 for the multiple classifier methods and weight parameter λ to 0.9. If we employ much member classifiers, the cost may be enough to select the best single classifier method, which would make our method discount. Therefore, the base classifiers should be employed as less as possible, but no downgrading the accuracy at the same time.

As shown in Fig. 6.1, the proposed method *CSGA_ACS* achieves the highest accuracies in all domains. Compared with the best single method, the accuracy of *CSGA_ACS* improves significantly, which means our method helps users get out of the trouble of selection difficulty on classifiers. Notably, the *avg_single* is much worse than the *best_single* in each domain, while it is often hard for users to select the best classifier without sufficient comparisons on all classifiers. Besides, for the two member classifier selection ways of *ACS*, namely *random_ACS* and *CSGA_ACS*, random selection is much worse than selecting member classifiers with *CSGA*. For the two classic ensemble learning methods, bagging and adaboost, their accuracies are worse than the best single classifier in all analyzed domains, even the accuracies of bagging are worse than the average accuracies of all optional classifiers in Apparels domain and Book domain. The reason is that these two methods use the same feature template, feature function, and classification algorithm in all iterations. Moreover, only part of labeled data sampled from the training set are used to train the classifiers in each iteration. Then, the accuracies of member classifiers are not high and the diversity among member classifiers is not obvious, which leads to the low performance of these two ways. Notably, the *bagging* and *adaboost* also counter the problem of selection difficulty on classifiers. In this experiment, different feature templates, feature functions, and classification algorithms are compared, and the best combination of these three basic factors is chosen.

The second experiment focuses on the comparison with the state art of *prune_eigcons* proposed in Ref. [Xu *et al.* (2012)], which formulated the selection of member classifiers as a constrained eigenvector problem and outperformed the other recent heuristics. As shown in Fig. 6.2, when the number of member classifiers is 5, our method overcomes the *prune_eigcons* in all analyzed domains. For the various number of member classifiers, we can observe that the accuracy curves of *CSGA_ACS* are above that of *prune_eigcons* for almost all locations, although these two curves tend to coincide with the increase of member classifier number. This means that *CSGA_ACS* can achieve earlier the best performance, which is important because training the member classifiers is time-consuming.

To compare the effectiveness of the proposed solution, *CSGA_ACS*, and the *Prune_Eigcons* further, we show their Receiver Operating Characteristic (ROC) curves for different domains in Fig. 6.3. In statistics, a ROC curve is a graphical

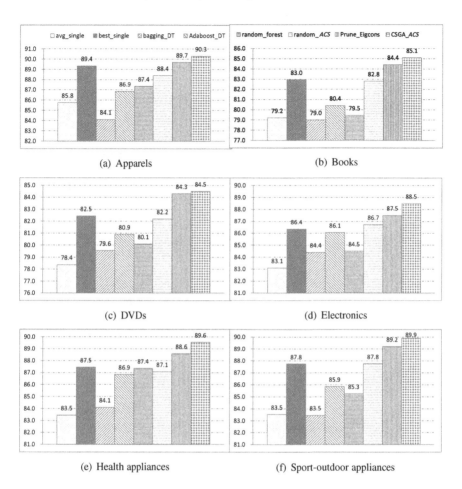

Fig. 6.1 Comparisons on accuracies (%) of different methods

plot that illustrates the performance of a binary classifier system as its discrimination threshold is varied, which is created by plotting the TPR (True Positive Rate) against the FPR (False Positive Rate) at various threshold setting. In ROC analysis, the area under the curve is used to measure the model's performance. In other words, the larger area under the ROC curve is, the better performance the model can achieve. As shown in Fig. 6.3, the ROC curves of *CSGA_ACS* locate over those of the *Prune_Eigcons* in all analyzed domains. It is clear that the *Prune_Eigcons* is also an effective way to generate predictions based on a set of classifiers for sentiment classification tasks. However, the *CSGA_ACS* can achieve the better performance in all analyzed domains.

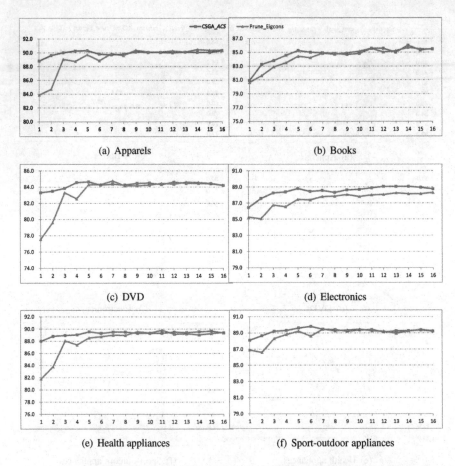

(a) Apparels   (b) Books

(c) DVD   (d) Electronics

(e) Health appliances   (f) Sport-outdoor appliances

Fig. 6.2   Varying the total number of member classifiers

Next, the assembling methods, *voting* and *ACS*, based on the *CSGA* are focused on. The *voting* is a straight and effective way to generate the final result for multiple optional results. As shown in Fig. 6.4, both *voting* and *ACS* are superior to the best single classifier method, but the final results generated by *ACS* are more accurate than those generated by *voting* in all analyzed domains.

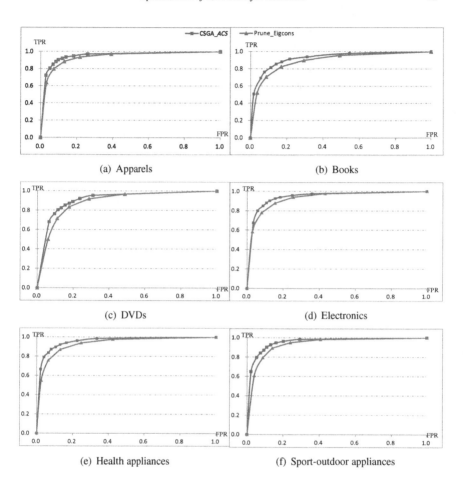

(a) Apparels   (b) Books

(c) DVDs   (d) Electronics

(e) Health appliances   (f) Sport-outdoor appliances

Fig. 6.3   The ROC curves of the CSGA_ACS and the *Prune_Eigcons*

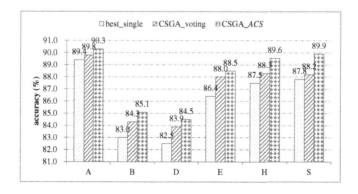

Fig. 6.4   Accuracy comparison of different assembling methods based on *CSGA*

The base classifiers are selected based on the their accuracies and diversity, which are controlled by the weight parameter λ. Figures 6.5(a) and 6.5(b) show the effect of λ for two assembling methods. The higher the λ is, the more contribution the accuracy will make according to the Equations 6.1 and 6.2. The main observation is that when the best performance of *voting* and *ACS* is achieved in most domains, the value of λ fall in the score of $[0.6, 0.9]$. This means that the accuracy plays a more important role in our solution. On the flip side, if the λ is set to 1, we cannot get the best performance. Then, the diversity serves as an effective complement.

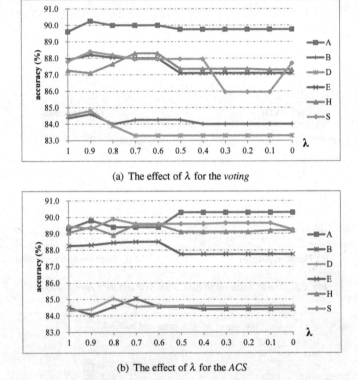

(a) The effect of λ for the *voting*

(b) The effect of λ for the *ACS*

Fig. 6.5   The effect of λ on accuracy for different assembling methods

In the last experiment, we consider the approximation ratio, which is the ratio of optimal value and approximation value, namely $\frac{optimal\_value}{approximation\_value}$. Firstly, we exhaust all possible member classifier combinations among the options and compute their object function values. The highest one is selected as the optimal value.

Secondly, we apply our *CSGA* to select the member classifiers and compute the corresponding object function value as the approximation value. The approximation ratios for all analyzed domains are shown in Table 6.1. We can see that the approximation ratios are very close to 1 for different λ value in all domains, although the upper bound of approximation is 2 as proven in Section 6.3. Notably, if the λ is set to 1, the approximation value is equal to the optimal value, that can be verified by the Equation 6.2 and Algorithm 6.1 directly.

Table 6.1 The approximation ratios with various λ values on different domains

$\lambda =$	1.0	0.9	0.8	0.7	0.6	0.5	0.4	0.3	0.2	0.1	0
A	1.00	1.00	1.00	1.01	1.02	1.02	1.03	1.04	1.05	1.07	1.09
B	1.00	1.00	1.00	1.00	1.01	1.01	1.00	1.00	1.00	1.00	1.01
D	1.00	1.01	1.01	1.00	1.00	1.00	1.01	1.01	1.01	1.02	1.02
E	1.00	1.00	1.01	1.01	1.01	1.02	1.02	1.03	1.04	1.05	1.06
H	1.00	1.00	1.00	1.01	1.01	1.02	1.03	1.04	1.05	1.07	1.09
S	1.00	1.00	1.00	1.00	1.00	1.01	1.01	1.02	1.02	1.03	1.04

6.5 Summary

This chapter focuses on the Combinatorial Explosion Problem of classifier set selection and proposes a greedy algorithm to choose the near optimal base classifiers. The time complexity of proposed algorithm is $O(n)$ for a relatively small k, where n is the count of optional base classifiers and k is the count of base classifiers chosen. Thus, the availability of three phase ensemble learning framework proposed in previous chapter is improved greatly. Moreover, the greedy algorithm is proven to be 2-approximation. The experiment results show that the approximation ratios are very close to 1 for different λ value in all domains, although the upper bound of approximation is 2. Therefore, the effectiveness of opinion analysis is guaranteed when the ensemble learning methods are used for such tasks.

Compared with the experiments in previous chapters, this chapter enlarges the scope of the analyzed domains. Multiple classic or new multiple classifier assembling technologies are compared with the proposed method. The experimental results show that the proposed method can achieve the best performance in all analyzed domains.

Chapter 7

Opinion spam detection

Online reviews have a significant influence on customers' purchasing decisions. This motivates some unscrupulous merchants to post fake reviews to mislead users by enhancing their reputation or diminishing the competitors. These fake reviews could mislead customers, which are often called opinion spam. Therefore, it brings an urgent demand to detect opinion spam as early as possible for reducing their negative impact.

We define the opinion spam as the reviews not expressing true experiences and opinions of users on corresponding products. Compared with other types of review spam defined in Ref. [Jindal and Liu (2007)], fake reviews are more harmful. Because it is very difficult for users to distinguish them from the normal ones, even for human readers [Ott *et al.* (2011); Lim *et al.* (2010)]. There are some prior works on spotting fake reviews such as Refs. [Ott *et al.* (2011); Jindal and Liu (2008); Lim *et al.* (2010); Mukherjee *et al.* (2012); Wang *et al.* (2012)], which have pushed the anti-opinion spam forward. However, their detection processes have ignored the orders of reviews. However, these works have ignored the posted order of reviews, which is important for the final target of online opinion spam detection. For instance, it would be difficult to determine whether the second example in Fig. 2.1 is a fake review, if the posted order of review is ignored. Thus, we focus on identifying fake reviews from the review sequence, which consists of a set of ordered reviews according to the posted time of review. This process is an essential procedure for implementing online opinion spam detection.

In this book, we focus on the problem of identifying the fake reviews from the review sequence. Our main idea is to highlight the fake reviews in the review sequence with the time sensitive features firstly based on the review contents and the reviewer behaviors. For example, a review spammer would post multiple reviews on several products to gain more benefits, and the malicious merchants would hire multiple spammers to post fake reviews on the target products in a relatively small time window to make a great influence. Secondly, we devise a supervised method and a threshold-based method to detect the fake reviews in the ordered review sequences separately. The former works well based on few labeled samples, and the latter also achieves fairly good effectiveness without labeled samples.

7.1 Highlighting the fake reviews

The fake reviews can be distinguished from the normal ones based on the review contents and the reviewer behaviors. For example, a fake review is probably the duplicate or near-duplicate of a normal review, a spammer prefers to post many reviews in a relatively short period for obtaining more benefits. In this section, we propose six features updated dynamically to highlight the review spam according to these two aspects.

7.1.1 *Modeling the review contents*

The spammers always take two main factors into account when they post fake reviews:

(1) In order to deceive the readers, the fake reviews should look like the normal ones.
(2) The fake reviews should be generated as quickly as possible to reduce the cost.

If a fake review is identified easily, it would not have a chance to mislead readers. On another front, spammers often post many fake reviews in a relatively short period in order to gain more benefits, while it will cost a lot (time or money) to write a normal review. Based on these two considerations, copying or making minor modifications on normal reviews is one of the most convenient ways to generate fake reviews. We divide the copied reviews into three types roughly: the reviews posted by the same spammer, the reviews on the same product, and the reviews on different products written by various reviewers. Thus, we can highlight the fake reviews from these three perspectives based on the review contents. Notably, these three types of reviews are likely to overlap. For example, a spammer copies a review written by himself to attack product A, with which he or she has commented on product B formerly.

Assuming $R = \{r[1], r[2], \ldots, r[n]\}$ is a review sequence[1], where the number means the posted order of review, the review $r[i](1 \leq i \leq n)$ contains multiple

---

[1]For simplicity, we only consider the case of the sequences with finite length in this paper. But the proposed methods can be used directly for the case of the sequences with infinite length.

information, such as reviewer ID $r[i].u$, posted time $r[i].t$, review content $r[i].c$ and target product ID $r[i].p$.

- *Personal content similarity* (F1)

If the reviewer $r[i].u$ copies his/her own reviews repeatedly, $r[i].c$ would have a relative high similarity with his/her reviews. We maintain a review centroid for each reviewer, which consists of terms' average occurrence frequencies in reviews posted by $r[i].u$. Thus, we can evaluate the personal content similarity of the detected review with the following equation.

$$S_u = similarity(r[i].c, \overline{C}_{r[i].u}) \tag{7.1}$$

where *similarity* is the function measuring text similarity like *cosine* similarity, $r[i].c$ is the content of the detected review, and $\overline{C}_{r[i].u}$ is the review content centroid of $r[i].u$. After review $r[i]$ is predicted, the centroid $\overline{C}_{r[i].u}$ is updated immediately.

- *Similarity with reviews on a product* (F2)

A fake review might be the duplicate or near-duplicate of an existing review on the same product, which the spammer wants to attack. By this way, the fake review is closely related to the product, and could achieve its goals of misleading readers at the same time. Once there are multiple reviews between the fake review and the normal ones copied, readers always cannot identify the fake review because most of them prefer to read the reviews in the first few pages.

Compared with the normal reviews, fake reviews would have higher similarity with the "average review" of product. Therefore, we can calculate the similarity of the detected review with those commenting on the same product as follows.

$$S_p = similarity(r[i].c, \overline{C}_{r[i].p}) \tag{7.2}$$

where $\overline{C}_{r[i].p}$ is the centroid of reviews on product $r[i].p$, which is similar to the $\overline{C}_{r[i].u}$. Similarly, the review centroid of a product would be updated after a review is processed.

- *Similarity with reviews on other products* (F3)

It is thorny to identify whether $r[i]$ is a duplicate or near-duplicate of $r[j]$ for all reviews on different products and $j < i$, when i is a big number, $r[i].p \neq r[j].p$ and $r[i].u \neq r[j].u$. Firstly, it is impracticable to calculate the similarity of $r[i].c$ with each $r[j].c$, because the total count of such review pairs would be very large. Secondly, if we apply the methods like F1 and F2, the discriminating components of centroid would tend to be 0 because of so many reviews. Therefore, we propose a solution for this case based on *minhashing* [Broder (1997)].

Given a string collection $S = \{o_1, \ldots, o_m\}$ and a hash function h, the *minhashing* value of S is defined as follows.

$$mh(S) = \arg\min_{o \in S}(h(o))$$

where the hash function h is used to permutate the elements in S randomly.

It is well known that there is a remarkable connection between *minhashing* and *Jaccard* similarity of the collections minhashed [Broder (1997)], namely,

$$Pr(mh(S_1) = mh(S_2)) = Jaccard(S_1, S_2).$$

Therefore, for a set of hash functions generated randomly, if each corresponding *minhashing* value of review $r[i].c$ is equal to that of review $r[j].c$, $r[i].c$ would be a duplicate of $r[j].c$ with relatively high probability.

Based on the discussions above, we apply *minhashing* on measuring the probability that the $r[i].c$ contains repeated contents in the collection of existing reviews. By this measurement, we can determine whether $r[i].c$ is a duplicate/near-duplicate of the existing review or not in a probabilistic sense. Firstly, we generate a set of d different hash functions $\{h_1, h_2, \ldots, h_d\}$ randomly. And then, we calculate the *minhashing* value for each hash function, and use these *minhashing* values to construct a hash signature for each review content ($r[i].c$), namely,

$$Sig(r[i].c) = H(mh_1(r[i].c), mh_2(r[i].c), \ldots, mh_d(r[i].c))$$

where H is a message-digest algorithm, which can generate a unique signature for a set of *minhashing* values. By this way, the comparison of two signatures is made conveniently.

The signatures of all reviews are maintained in a signature set. If the signature of $r[i].c$ already exists in this signature set, $r[i].c$ would be a duplicate or near-duplicate with very high probability. But if the signature of $r[i].c$ does not exists in this signature set, there will be two scenarios:

(1) $r[i].c$ is not a duplicate or near-duplicate.
(2) $r[i].c$ is a near-duplicate of a certain review content. Without loss of generality, we assume $r[i].c$ is the near-duplicate of $r[j].c$ (j¡i). But a few *minhashing* values of $r[i].c$ are different from those of $r[j].c$.

For the second scenario, we can generate multiple signatures for each review by repeating the processes above. Thus, even if one of signatures of $r[i].c$ is different from those of $r[j].c$, other signatures of $r[i].c$ might be the same with those of $r[j].c$. The more times they are the same, $r[i].c$ will be more likely to be a near-duplicate of $r[j].c$.

Formally, let $h_{i1}, h_{i2}, \ldots, h_{id}$ ($i = 1, 2, \ldots, b$) denote b sets of *hash* functions, which would generate different random permutations. The $H_1, H_2, \ldots, H_b$ denote

b signature sets respectively. Thus, the probability of $r[i].c$ be a duplicate or near-duplicate which can be evaluated as follows.

$$S_O = \frac{\sum_{i=1}^{b} exist(Sig_i)}{b}, \tag{7.3}$$

$$exist(Sig_i) = \begin{cases} 1 & Sig_i \in H_i, \\ 0 & Sig_i \notin H_i. \end{cases}$$

The above processes are described in Algorithm 7.1. The signature sets $H_1, H_2, \ldots, H_b$ maintained in previous detection procedure serve as the input of next detection. We calculate a *minhashing* value for each random arrangement (line 6). Then we will get d *minhashing* values, and all of these values are connected to form a string (line 7). Based on this string, a *minhashing* signature of $r[i].c$ is generated (line 9). At last, we check whether the signature exists in the corresponding signature set, and predict the review's label accordingly (line 10–13).

Algorithm 7.1 *Minhashing* duplicate/near-duplicate probability

---

Input: review $r[i]$,
       signature sets $H_1, H_2, \ldots, H_b$,
       the set of b groups of hash functions $\{(h_{11}, h_{12}, \ldots, h_{1d}),$
       $\ldots, (h_{b1}, h_{b2}, \ldots, h_{bd})\}$
Output: the probability that $r[i].c$ is a duplicate or near-duplicate
1: $count = 0$;
2: generate the n-gram set $S_{r[i]}$ for $r[i].c$;
3: **for** $i = 1$ TO b **do**
4:     $hashStr = null$;
5:     **for** $j = 1$ TO d **do**
6:        $mh = \arg\min_{s \in S_{r[i]}} (h_{ij}(S_{r[i]}))$;
7:        $hashStr = hashStr + mh$; //connect all *minhashing* values.
8:     **end for**
9:     $sig = strHash(hashStr)$; //The $strHash$ is a signature function.
10:    **if** $sig \in H_i$ **then**
11:       $count = count + 1$;
12:    **else**
13:       $H_i = H_i \bigcup \{sig\}$;
14:    **end if**
15: **end for**
16: **return** $count/b$;

7.1.2 *Modeling the reviewer behaviors*

Some behaviors of spammers could also imply that the reviews posted by them are fake reviews, such as a spammer posts multiple reviews in a short period of time, such reviews are likely to be fake review. Thus, we can model such behaviors to highlight the fake reviews.

- *The review frequency of reviewer* (F4)

If the posted time of $r[i]$ is very close to the previous review time of $r[i].u$, $r[i]$ may be a fake review, because spammers prefer to post many fake reviews in a short time in order to gain more benefits. Thus, we can evaluate a review's probability of being a fake review by the time interval between two consecutive posted time for the same reviewer.

$$S_{uf} = 1 - \frac{I_u[pre(r[i].u), r[i].t]}{\max(I_u)} \tag{7.4}$$

where $pre(r[i].u)$ is the latest review time of $r[i].u$, $r[i].t$ is the posted time of review $r[i]$, $I_u[x, y]$ is the time interval between x and y, and $\max(I_u)$ is the maximum time interval among all pairs of adjacent reviews posted by $r[i].u$.

- *The review frequency of a product* (F5)

The influence of single fake review is limited, but multiple fake reviews occurring in a short time interval will have greater impact. If a product is commented very frequently with a burst mode, it might be attacked by fake reviews. Of course, such case could be caused by other reasons, such as promotions. But we also treat it as an index of spammer's behavior.

$$S_{pf} = 1 - \frac{I_p[pre(r[i].p), r[i].t]}{\max(I_p)} \tag{7.5}$$

where $pre(r[i].p)$ is the latest review time on product $r[i].p$, $I_p[x, y]$ is the same with that defined in Equation 7.4, but x and y are the posted time of two reviews on the same product respectively, and $\max(I_p)$ is the maximum time interval among all pairs of adjacent reviews on product $r[i].p$.

- *The repeatability measure* (F6)

Review spammers might comment a product repeatedly. Supposing the review $r[i]$ is a fake review. If $r[i]$ has a long interval with the last review posted by $r[i].u$, the feature F4 would not highlight this spam behavior. On the other hand, if $r[i].p$ is a very popular product, it will be commented frequently, and the feature F5 does not work. Therefore, we make a complement for F4 and F5 with checking whether $r[i].u$ has commented $r[i].p$ or not.

$$S_r = \begin{cases} 1 & r[i].u \in U_p \\ 0 & r[i].u \notin U_p \end{cases} \tag{7.6}$$

where U_p is the collection of reviewers, who have commented product $r[i].p$.

7.2 The fake review detection methods

From the aspects of review contents and reviewer behaviors, we can distinguish the fake reviews from the normal ones. Thus, the fake review detection tasks can be viewed as a binary classification issue, in which a review will be classified as "normal" or "spam".

7.2.1 Problem definition

For an ordered review sequence $R = \{r[1], r[2], \ldots, r[n]\}$ and the label set $L = \{L_{normal}, L_{spam}\}$, the reviews with label L_{normal} are the normal reviews, and those with label L_{spam} are the fake reviews.

The fake review detection targets at finding a function D, which predicts the label of each review one by one according to the appearance order of reviews:

$$\hat{L}_{r[i]} = D(r[i]) \tag{7.7}$$

where $r[i] \in R$ and $\hat{L}_{r[i]} \in L$.

Based on the six features proposed above, we can transform the review $r[i] (1 \leq i \leq n)$ into a vector X_i, and apply the supervised methods and the threshold-based one to predict the label of this review.

7.2.2 The supervised detection methods

Given a labeled review collection $T = \{(X_1, y_1), \ldots, (X_n, y_n)\}$, where $y_i \in L$ ($1 \leq i \leq n$) is the true label of X_i. Based on these labeled samples, we can apply Logistic regression or SVM to make predictions.

For Logistic regression, the parameter vector $\hat{\omega}$ can be evaluated by Maximum Likelihood Estimations. Thus, the Logistic regression model for fake review detection can be defined as follows.

$$P(y = L_{spam}|X) = \frac{\exp(\hat{\omega} \cdot X)}{1 + \exp(\hat{\omega} \cdot X)}$$

$$P(y = L_{normal}|X) = \frac{1}{1 + \exp(\hat{\omega} \cdot X)}$$

We also predict the review labels with trained SVM classifier, which tries to find a high-dimensional separating hyperplane between two groups of data. To simplify feature analysis in later section, we restrict our evaluation to *linear* SVM, which learns a weight vector $\hat{\omega}$ and bias term b, such that a review X_j can be classified by:

$$\hat{y} = sign(\hat{\omega} \cdot X_j + \hat{b})$$

It is worth noting that we need to update the corresponding centroids for F1 and F2, the signature sets for F3, the maximum time intervals for F4 and F5 and the comment status of each product for F6, after each review is processed.

7.2.3 *The threshold-based detection method*

Although the classifiers trained by labeled samples have stronger generalization ability, the procedure of labeling samples is time-consuming and error-prone. More importantly, the fake reviews make up only a small proportion of all reviews. Thus, it would take some time to gather a certain amount of fake reviews to train the classifiers. Before we have collected the enough training samples, the fake reviews would make negative influence and it is possible that some users would make their decisions based on the fake reviews.

Therefore, we devise a threshold-based solution for detecting fake reviews without labeled samples. Recalled the features F1–F6 discussed in Section 7.1, each of them tries to highlight the fake reviews from different perspectives. Intuitively, if a review is a spam, the sum of the feature values of F1–F6 would tend to be close to 6, because all of them locate in $[0, 1]$ according to their definitions. Thus, we can evaluate the spam score of a review by the following equation:

$$Score = \frac{(a_1 S_u + a_2 S_p + a_3 S_O + a_4 S_{uf} + a_5 S_{pf} + a_6 S_r)}{\sum_{k=1}^{6} a_k} \quad (7.8)$$

where $a_1, a_2, \ldots, a_6$ are the weight parameters turning the contributions of feature F1, F2, $\ldots$, F6 separately.

In Equation 7.8, the spam score of a review is normalized in $[0, 1]$. Therefore, we can detect review spam with a predetermined threshold τ, such as 0.5:

$$L_{r[i]} = \begin{cases} L_{normal} & Score_{r[i]} < \tau \\ L_{spam} & Score_{r[i]} > \tau \\ random & Score_{r[i]} = \tau \end{cases} \quad (7.9)$$

where the *random* means selecting a label from $\{L_{normal}, L_{spam}\}$ as the label of $r[i]$ randomly.

Similarly, the two corresponding centriods, two maximum time intervals, the signature sets, and comment status will be updated immediately after each review is detected.

7.3 Experiments

In this section, we construct an ordered review spam dataset with the Amazon reviews firstly. Based on this dataset, we verify the effectiveness of the fake review detection methods proposed in Section 7.2.

7.3.1 *Dataset construction and evaluation criterias*

One of the main challenges encountered by fake review detection is the absence of ground-truth, because fake reviews are difficult to determine, even for human readers. The common methods for labeling fake reviews include two types: manual labeling such as in Ref. [Li *et al.* (2011); Lim *et al.* (2010)] and treating the duplicates/near-duplicates of reviews as the fake ones such as in Ref. [Jindal and Liu (2007, 2008)]. The former is time-consuming and error prone. Thus, we apply the second method to reconstruct our fake review dataset with the following processes based on Liu's review dataset[2],which was crawled from Amazon:

(1) Removing the reviews on the inactive products, and keeping the products with review number is greater than or equal to 10.
(2) Sorting the reviews of each product according to their posted time. But the posted time granularity of review is day in Liu's dataset, we crawl the reviews of the products commented multiple times in a day from Amazon with the displaying model "Newest First", and sort the reviews in Liu's dataset according to this order on Amazon for each product. By this way, we can determine the arrival order of every review.
(3) Calculating the *Jaccard* similarity of each pair reviews for bigrams on a cluster.
(4) Labeling the reviews as fake reviews, whose *Jaccard* similarity is greater than or equal to 0.7, the others are marked as normal reviews.
(5) Sorting each pairs of reviewer with high *Jaccard* similarity (≥ 0.7) according to their posted orders, the review posted early locates before the later ones. And then, the relative copy behaviors construct an order chain. We remark the reviews as the normal reviews at the first locations of all copy chains, because we cannot be sure whether they are duplicates or near-duplicates in our review dataset.

We have collected 2000 fake reviews with these processes above together with corresponding normal reviews based on Liu's dataset. All of these reviews are

---

[2]https://www.cs.uic.edu/~liub/FBS/sentiment-analysis.html

sorted by the posted time, which constitute an ordered review dataset. Table 7.1 shows some statistical information on the reconstructed review dataset.

Table 7.1   Some statistical information on the reconstructed review dataset

Reviewed products	Reviews	Reviewers	Review spam
6824	155080	122672	2000

For the reconstructed review dataset, we find that most products attacked by spammers have no more than 3 fake reviews. Figure 7.1 shows the number of fake reviews vs. the number of products, the relationship between them follows the power law distribution basically. The reviewed product attacked most times has 34 fake reviews in our reconstructed dataset, whose ID on Amazon is 0140177396.[3]

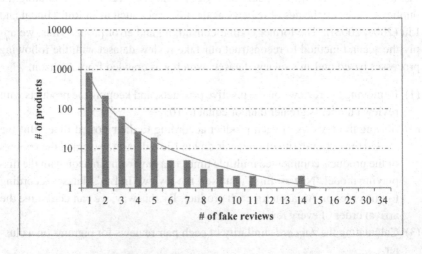

Fig. 7.1   The distribution of reviews in products

In this chapter, we try to detect fake reviews from the review sequence with the supervised methods and the threshold-based one based on six features proposed in Section 7.1. The Logistic regression[4] and SVM[5] are treated as the supervised classification algorithms respectively. To measure the effectiveness of fake review

---

[3]http://www.amazon.com/Of-Mice-Men-John-Steinbeck/dp/0140177396/ref=sr_1_1?ie=UTF8&qid =1380962501&sr=8-1&keywords=0140177396

[4]We implement the Logistic regression with WEKA. http://www.weka.net.nz

[5]We implement the SVM with LIBSVM. http://www.csie.ntu.edu.tw/~cjlin/libsvm/

detection, the *accuracy* is treated as one of the evaluation criterias:

$$accuracy = \frac{tp + tn}{tp + tn + fp + fn}$$

where tp is the number of fake reviews detected correctly, tn is the number of normal reviews detected correctly, fp is the number of normal reviews predicted as fake reviews erroneously, and fn is the number of fake reviews predicted as normal reviews erroneously.

However, it is not enough to consider the detection accuracy only, because fake reviews are a very tiny proportion of all reviews in our dataset. Thus, if we predict all reviews to be the normal ones, the prediction *accuracy* is still very high. But it is completely useless for users, since our main target is to find the fake reviews. Therefore, we treat the *precision*, *recall* and *F1-score* on fake review detection as the important indexes:

$$precision_s = \frac{tp}{tp + fp}$$

$$recall_s = \frac{tp}{tp + fn}$$

$$F_1(s) = 2 \times \frac{precision_s \times recall_s}{precision_s + recall_s}$$

For both of the supervised methods and the threshold-based method, we need to predetermine the number (b) of signature sets and the number (d) of hash functions for a hash signature in order to calculate the value of F3, which are set empirically. In our experiments, b is set to be 8 and d to be 4, both of them need to be tuned. For the LIBSVM, we apply linear kernel, and the other parameter are kept the default values.

Notably, we are not able to compare our solutions with the others proposed in some prior works like Refs. [Jindal and Liu (2007); Li *et al.* (2011)], because of the following two main reasons:

(1) The solutions proposed in this Chapter are sensitive to the posted orders of reviews, which is crucial for implementing the online opinion spam detection. But prior works on this problem have ignored the review orders, they focus on detecting the review spam in a review set accumulated over long periods of time.

(2) Some features used by prior works cannot be obtained when we detect the review as soon as they arrive, such as the number of helpful feedbacks and the average rating of product.

7.3.2 *Experimental results and discussion*

In this subsection, we carry out a series of experiments to verify the effectiveness of the solutions on fake review detection presented in Section 7.2 based on the proposed six features.

For the supervised detection, we need to label the reviews to train the classifiers. The labeled samples would be chosen according to the posted orders of reviews, because we target at proposing the online solution for fake review detection. In this way, we can simulate the arrival order of reviews in real-word, and avoid to use the later reviews to predict the labels of the front ones.

The first experiment focuses on the detection effectiveness of fake reviews in the case of balance training samples, namely, the number of fake reviews is equal to that of normal reviews. Table 7.2 shows the result comparisons of fake review detection with SVM based on different numbers of training samples in the balance training model. When the number of training samples is changed, we can observe that all detection accuracies are very high ($> 99\%$). That is because the number of fake reviews is very small. When we use 50 fake reviews and 50 normal reviews to train the SVM classifier, we get the maximum $F_1(s)$ value (0.852) in this experiment. In this case, most fake reviews are identified, and the *precision* on fake reviews is relatively high (close to 80%). Therefore, we just need to collect a few of fake reviews to train the classifier, we would achieve a good performance. This is very important, because collecting fake reviews is time-consuming, which would provide spammers chances to attack in this period.

Table 7.2   The effect of review spam detection with SVM based on balance training samples

	# of training samples						
	50	100	150	200	300	400	500
accuracy	0.994	0.996	0.994	0.993	0.995	0.995	0.995
$precision_s$	0.699	0.790	0.678	0.669	0.743	0.735	0.728
$recall_s$	0.933	0.924	0.947	0.948	0.948	0.947	0.976
$F_1(s)$	0.799	**0.852**	0.790	0.785	0.833	0.828	0.834

The Logistic regression works poorly with the balance training samples due to overfitting, because the true distribution of fake reviews in our dataset is extreme imbalance. For instance, if we use 50 fake reviews and 50 normal reviews to train the Logistic regression model for classification, the $precision_s$ is 0.033, $recall_s$ is 0.965 and $F_1(s)$ is 0.065. This means much normal reviews are predicted as fake reviews mistakenly. The main reason is that Logistic regression determines the location of decision plane with the sum of the distance between two types of training samples, while SVM depends on only a few of support vectors. Thus, the SVM has stronger generalization capability compared with the Logistic regression in this experiment.

We focus on the case of the unbalance training samples in the next experiment. The count of fake reviews for training is fix, and we compare the effectiveness of fake review detection with different proportions of fake reviews and normal ones for training by increasing the quantity of normal reviews gradually. In this experiment, we use 50 fake reviews and $50 \times i$ ($2 \leq i \leq 20$) normal reviews to train the classifier, the remaining reviews in our dataset are treated as testing samples. Figure 7.2 shows the comparisons on $F_1(s)$ of Logistic regression and SVM for fake review detection with the unbalance training samples. The detection effects of both methods are improved, when the number of normal reviews is increased until the number is 700. When we apply 50 fake reviews and 800 normal reviews for training, the SVM achieves the highest *F1(spam)* value (0.923), and the detection *precision* on spam is 0.939, the *recall* of spam is 0.908. Moreover, we can observe that the SVM is not very sensitive to the count of normal reviews, namely, its performance changes little with the increase of normal review quantity. Moreover, the performance of the Logistic-based method is changed significantly before it becomes stable, especially for the range of normal review number from 600 to 700. Notably, the $F_1(s)$ of SVM with less training samples can be close to the best $F_1(s)$ of Logistic regression, that means SVM would start to work effectively earlier, while the latter needs to collect more labeled samples for training to achieve the same effectiveness. Thus, the detection method based on SVM would reduce the chances of damage caused by fake reviews.

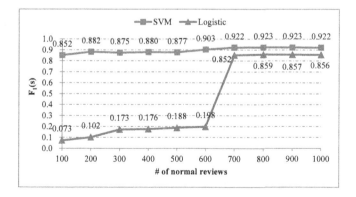

Fig. 7.2   The effectiveness of fake review detection with unbalance samples

We construct six features to find the fake reviews by modeling review contents and reviewer behaviors, the supervised detection method can achieve a good effectiveness based on these features in previous experiments.

Table 7.3   The contributions of six features for fake review detection

Feature option	$precision_s$	$recall_s$	$F_1(s)$
111111	0.939	0.908	**0.923**
011111	0.884	0.914	0.899
101111	0.927	0.902	0.914
110111	0.907	0.747	0.819
111011	0.937	0.910	**0.923**
111101	0.938	0.905	0.921
111110	0.940	0.900	0.920
111000	0.907	0.864	0.885
000111	0.802	0.661	0.725

For the contributions of the proposed features to fake review detection, Table 7.3 shows the identification results of the SVM-based method with different feature options respectively, in which 50 fake reviews and 800 normal reviews are used to train. According to the order from F1 to F6, the "1" indicates the feature in corresponding location would be used, and "0" means the feature would not be used. For example, the "111111" denotes we use all of the six features, and the "110111" denotes we use the proposed features, except the feature F3.

As shown in Table 7.3, the feature F1, F2, F3, F5 and F6 play the active roles in fake review detection processes, because if we remove any one of them, it will lead to the declining effectiveness. When we omit the feature F4, the $F_1(s)$ values are not changed. Recalled the definition of F4 in Section 7.1, it indicates that the smaller time interval between the posted time of a review and that of the previous one wrote by the corresponding reviewer, the greater probability of being fake the review has. But the time granularity of review is the day in our dataset, while some normal reviewers also write multiple reviews in one day. Thus, we cannot distinguish the spammers' behaviors from the normal reviewers' by this way. Although the posted frequency of spammer is much higher than that of the normal reviewer, since a normal reviewer need to denote more time on writing a review manually, while a spammer prefers to post the duplicates or near-duplicates of the existing reviews. This may be the main reason that the feature F4 does not work. If we could obtain the review posted time with finer granularity, we consider that the feature F4 would make its contribution to fake review detection. The last two rows in Table 7.3 are the effectiveness of considering only review contents or reviewer behaviors separately. The main observation is that the review content is more efficient than the reviewer behavior for fake review detection. We consider that the main reason is still the time granularity. Interestingly, when we only use the features based on the reviewer behaviors, the effectiveness of the Logistic-based method will be very close to that of the SVM-based method.

The experiments above show that the supervised detection methods can achieve the good effectiveness based on a few of training samples. But it still takes some time to collect the fake reviews for training, because the fake review remains a tiny proportion of all reviews. Thus, we propose an threshold-based detection method to identify the fake reviews in the review sequence, which is verified in the following experiment.

For the threshold-based method, we need to predetermine two sets of parameters: the feature weights in Equation 7.8 and the threshold τ in Equation 7.9. Table 7.4 lists the effectiveness of the threshold-based method with different parameter combinations, where the weights of six proposed features are set in the second column. For instance, the "212111" means the weights of F1 and F3 are 2 respectively, and those of others are 1. In Equation 7.8, we normalize the review spam score in $[0, 1]$. Intuitively, if a review is fake, the sum of its six feature values would prefer to be 1, otherwise to be 0. Thus, the ideal threshold τ should be 0.5. But we would get the highest value of $F_1(s)$ with the $\tau = 0.55$ and the feature weight setting "212111", which is very close to that of the supervised Logistic-based method with 50 fake reviews and 700 normal reviews for training. Meanwhile, if the feature values based on review contents are larger than those that are based on reviewer behaviors in this experiment, we will get the better effectiveness.

Moreover, with the increase of τ, the *precision_s* is increasing and the *recall_s* is decreasing for the same set of parameters. Therefore, we can turn the threshold τ to reach various effectiveness for different applications. For example, when we need to filter the fake reviews as many as possible, we should set the τ to be relatively small. If we have more stringent detection precision on fake reviews, we should apply relatively large τ.

7.4 Summary

Online reviews are very important for many e-commerce applications, because they contain rich user opinions and experiences. These user-generated contents are essential for Word Of Mouth (WOM) on Web, by which users can also make

Table 7.4 The effectiveness of the threshold-based detection method

	Feature option	accuracy	precision$_s$	recall$_s$	$F_1(s)$
$\tau = 0.50$	111111	0.995	0.804	0.791	0.797
	212112	0.995	0.829	0.799	0.814
	212111	0.996	0.875	0.821	0.847
$\tau = 0.55$	111111	0.995	0.822	0.755	0.787
	212112	0.996	0.873	0.780	0.824
	212111	0.996	0.916	0.796	**0.851**
$\tau = 0.60$	111111	0.995	0.867	0.742	0.800
	212112	0.996	0.916	0.753	0.827
	212111	0.996	0.935	0.773	0.846

the appropriate decisions. Driven by interests, some dishonest users apply opinion spam to mislead the others by posting the fake reviews, which would damage the normal users' benefits seriously. Therefore, fake review detection has received a great deal of attention in recent years. But most of the existing works focus on detecting fake review detection in a review collection, and the posted orders of reviews have been neglected. But this posted order is vital for implementing the online anti-opinion spam.

In this chapter, we explore the problem of identifying fake reviews from the review sequence, which is made up of the ordered reviews according to their posted time. Firstly, we highlight the fake reviews with six time sensitive features based on modeling the review contents and the reviewer behaviors. Secondly, we devise the supervised method and the threshold-based one for fake review detection respectively. And then, we construct an ordered labeled review set based on Amazon reviews. At last, we carry out a series of experiments to verify the effectiveness of the proposed methods on the constructed real-world dataset, and analyze the utilities of the six proposed features in different cases. The experimental results show that the supervised methods can work with high precision and recall on fake reviews based on a small amount of training samples, and the threshold-based one can achieve a relatively good effectiveness without training samples.

Chapter 8

Conclusions

The user-generated contents play a more and more important role in Web applications. Online review is one of the most valuable parts of such contents, since it is opinion-rich. Many new intelligence systems and applications such as e-commerce/e-government, public opinion monitoring and recommender system must depend on the analysis of these data. Automatic identification of the opinions expressed in online reviews is one key point for the success of such systems and applications. Therefore, opinion analysis on online reviews has attracted more and more attention recently.

Machine learning is an effective way to analyze the opinions expressed in online reviews automatically, which is introduced in detail in this book's introduction. Three main contributions are made:

(1) The traditional text classification technologies do not consider the sentiment of terms, which leads to poor performances for opinion analysis tasks. A new feature presentation is proposed for opinion task, which integrates the terms' sentiment and contribution to review. This method can not only evaluate the sentiment of *unigram*, but also *n-gram* ($n > 1$). This is not supported by the general sentiment dictionaries. The feature presentation with sentiment information of terms improves the classification accuracy on opinion analysis compared to the traditional feature presentations.

(2) When the machine learning methods are applied on opinion analysis, users always need to determine three basic factors of a classifier: feature type, feature function and classification algorithm. The combination of such basic factors has a great influence on the performance of a classifier. However, the classifier with best performance is a variable for different analyzed domains, since each one has its own characteristic. Thus, it is always hard to choose the optimal classifier. Furthermore, how to improve the performance of opinion analysis based on the available classifiers is a valuable research. The ensemble

learning method is introduced for opinion analysis. A three phase ensemble learning framework is proposed, in which the optimal set of classifiers is chosen automatically based on the accuracies and diversity of base classifiers. To assemble the base classifiers, an algorithm based on stacking technology is proposed. Our solution not only solves the problem of classifier selection, but also achieves a better performance on opinion analysis than the single classifier methods.

(3) If the number of optional classifiers are small, the quality evaluating metric can acquire the optimal set of base classifiers. Unfortunately, when the number of candidates improves, it will encounter the Combinatorial Explosion Problem of classifiers. This limits the availability and scalability of multiple classifier ensemble learning framework. For this limitation, the selection issue of classifier set is converted to an optimization problem. A greedy algorithm is devised for the selection of base classifiers, which is proved to be 2-approximation. Thus, the quality of base classifier chosen is reliable. At the same time, the time complexity of the proposed greedy algorithm is $O(n)$, where n is the number of optional classifiers. The experiment results show that the set of base classifiers can achieve a good performance in the ensemble learning framework, and the object function value of base classifiers is very close to the optimal one.

The online review is one of the main objects on opinion analysis. For the proposed methods above, extensive experiments are carried out on real-world datasets. Because opinion words are related to the domain, the proposed methods are compared with different methods in multiple domains. The experiment results show that our methods achieve the best performance.

The emergence of social media has given Web users a platform to contribute contents for expressing and sharing their thoughts and opinions on what they care. These user-generated contents account for a large proportion of Web data, which contains rich user opinions. As an important kind of semantic words, user opinions should be identified correctly in order to match the demand of semantic understanding in Web3.0 age. A lots of opinion analysis techniques have been proposed to identify users' opinions in the past decade. Most of these techniques focus on some special problems and applications. In other words, the basic techniques on opinion analysis have been gradually perfected. However, users' opinion hides in unstructured texts, which restrains the automatic use of opinion knowledge. Therefore, a following important problem is about how to utilize such opinion knowledge efficiently. At first, the opinion knowledge should be identified and extracted from massive documents. And then, they would be organized into an unitized and structured framework. Moreover, users' social relationship should also be integrated into this framework, because a user's opinions could be affected by his/her friends. Besides, an ontology of opinion categories developed by Semantic Web technologies like Resource Description Framework (RDF) and Ontology Web Language (OWL) could improve the performance of opinion analysis system, by which we can get an uniform understanding on the concepts of opinions.

In summary, users play core roles on Web. Analyzing user's opinions is a key step to match user's demands. In spite of much works on opinion analysis, there are still many challenges in this area:

(1) The traditional machine learning techniques work in relatively small datasets. In the case of massive data, the existing techniques face serious challenges. It brings an urgent requirement to explore new techniques for opinion analysis to deal with the large scale datasets.

(2) Most of existing studies on opinion analysis focus on the isolated objects. How do the opinions spread on the social network? What are the spreading models? Which nodes are the key ones in the spreading process? Such problems need to be further explored.

(3) Opinion analysis depends on the strong computing power of computer, however, the ability of human is ignored. Now many crowdsourcing platforms have increasingly improved, hence, how to improve the performance of opinion analysis by leveraging the ability of human is an interesting problem.

(4) The opinions are expressed in unstructured text. How to model, clean, store and retrieval the massive opinion data uniformly is worth to explore further.

Bibliography

Agarwal, A., Xie, B., Vovsha, I., Rambow, O., and Passonneau, R. (2011). Sentiment analysis of twitter data, in *Proceedings of the Workshop on Languages in Social Media* (Association for Computational Linguistics), pp. 30–38.

Alm, C. O., Roth, D., and Sproat, R. (2005). Emotions from text: machine learning for text-based emotion prediction, in *Proceedings of the conference on Human Language Technology and Empirical Methods in Natural Language Processing* (Association for Computational Linguistics), pp. 579–586.

Andreevskaia, A. and Bergler, S. (2006). Mining wordnet for a fuzzy sentiment: Sentiment tag extraction from wordnet glosses, in *Proceedings of the conference on European Chapter of the Association for Computational Linguistics*, pp. 209–216.

Baccianella, S., Esuli, A., and Sebastiani, F. (2010). Sentiwordnet 3.0: An enhanced lexical resource for sentiment analysis and opinion mining, in *Proceedings of the ninth international conference on Language Resources and Evaluation*, Vol. 10 (European Language Resources Association (ELRA)), pp. 2200–2204.

Barbosa, L. and Feng, J. (2010). Robust sentiment detection on twitter from biased and noisy data, in *Proceedings of the 23rd International Conference on Computational Linguistics: Posters* (Association for Computational Linguistics), pp. 36–44.

Barbosa, L. and Feng, J. (2011). Target-dependent twitter sentiment classification, in *Proceedings of the 49th annual meeting on Association for Computational Linguistics* (Association for Computational Linguistics), pp. 151–160.

Bautin, M., Vijayarenu, L., and Skiena, S. (2008). International sentiment analysis for news and blogs, in *Proceedings of the Second International Conference on Weblogs and Social Media.*, pp. 19–26.

Blitzer, J., Dredze, M., and Pereira, F. (2007). Biographies, bollywood, boom-boxes and blenders: Domain adaptation for sentiment classification, in *Proceedings of the 45th Annual Meeting of the Association of Computational Linguistics*, Vol. 7, pp. 440–447.

Borodin, A., Lee, H. C., and Ye, Y. (2012). Max-sum diversification, monotone submodular functions and dynamic updates, in *Proceedings of the 31st symposium on Principles of Database Systems* (ACM), pp. 155–166.

Breiman, L., Friedman, J., Stone J. C. and Olshen, R. A. (1984). Classification and regression trees (Chapman and Hall).

Brin, S. and Page, L. (1998). The anatomy of a large-scale hypertextual web search engine, *Computer networks and ISDN systems* **30**, 1, pp. 107–117.

Broder, A. Z. (1997). On the resemblance and containment of documents, in *Proceedings of the Compression and Complexity of Sequences* (IEEE), pp. 21–29.

Chen, F., Han, K., and Chen, G. (2002). An approach to sentence-selection-based text summarization, in *TENCON'02 Proceedings, 2002 IEEE Region 10 Conference on Computers, Communications, Control and Power Engineering*, Vol. 1 (IEEE), pp. 489–493.

Cortes, C. and Vapnik, V. (1995). Support-vector networks, *Machine learning* **20**, 3, pp. 273–297.

Cui, H., Mittal, V., and Datar, M. (2006). Comparative experiments on sentiment classification for online product reviews, in *AAAI*, Vol. 6, pp. 1265–1270.

Danescu-Niculescu-Mizil, C., Kossinets, G., Kleinberg, J., and Lee, L. (2009). How opinion are received by online communities: a case study on amazon.com helpfulness votes, in *Proceedings of the 18th international conference on World wide web* (ACM), pp. 141–150.

Dasgupta, S. and Ng, V. (2009). Mine the easy, classify the hard: a semi-supervised approach to automatic sentiment classification, in *Proceedings of the Joint Conference of the 47th Annual Meeting of the ACL and the 4th International Joint Conference on Natural Language Processing of the AFNLP: Volume 2-Volume 2* (Association for Computational Linguistics), pp. 701–709.

Dave, K., Lawrence, S., and Pennock, D. M. (2003). Mining the peanut gallery: Opinion extraction and semantic classification of product reviews, in *Proceedings of the 12th international conference on World Wide Web* (ACM), pp. 519–528.

Džeroski, S. and Ženko, B. (2004). Is combining classifiers with stacking better than selecting the best one? *Machine learning* **54**, 3, pp. 255–273.

Erkan, G. and Radev, D. R. (2004). Lexrank: Graph-based lexical centrality as salience in text summarization, *Journal of Artificial Intelligence Research* **22**, 1, pp. 457–479.

Esuli, A. and Sebastiani, F. (2005). Determining the semantic orientation of terms through gloss classification, in *Proceedings of the 14th ACM International Conference on Information and Knowledge Management* (ACM), pp. 617–624.

Esuli, A. and Sebastiani, F. (2006a). Determining term subjectivity and term orientation for opinion mining, in *Conference on European Chapter of the Association for Computational Linguistics* (Association for Computational Linguistics), pp. 193–200.

Esuli, A. and Sebastiani, F. (2006b). Sentiwordnet: A publicly available lexical resource for opinion mining, in *Proceedings of the fifth international conference on Language Resources and Evaluation*, Vol. 6 (European Language Resources Association (ELRA)), pp. 417–422.

Etzioni, O., Cafarella, M., Downey, D., Popescu, A.-M., Shaked, T., Soderland, S., Weld, D. S., and Yates, A. (2005). Unsupervised named-entity extraction from the web: An experimental study, *Artificial Intelligence* **165**, 1, pp. 91–134.

Feng, S., Wang, D., Yu, G., Gao, W., and Kam-Fai, W. (2011). Extracting common emotions from blogs based on fine-grained sentiment clustering, *Knowledge and information systems* **27**, 2, pp. 281–302.

Fleiss, J. L., Levin, B., and Paik, M. C. (2013). *Statistical methods for rates and proportions* (John Wiley & Sons).

Gamon, M. (2004). Sentiment classification on customer feedback data: Noisy data, large feature vectors, and the role of linguistic analysis, in *Proceedings of the 20th international conference on Computational Linguistics* (Association for Computational Linguistics), p. 841.

Gamon, M. and Aue, A. (2005). Automatic identification of sentiment vocabulary: exploiting low association with known sentiment terms, in *Proceedings of the ACL Workshop on Feature Engineering for Machine Learning in Natural Language Processing* (Association for Computational Linguistics), pp. 57–64.

Ghose, A. and Ipeirotis, P. G. (2007). Designing novel review ranking systems: predicting the usefulness and impact of reviews, in *Proceedings of the ninth international conference on electronic commerce* (ACM), pp. 303–310.

Go, A., Bhayani, R., and Huang, L. (2009). Twitter sentiment classification using distant supervision, *CS224N Project Report, Stanford*, pp. 1–12.

Gunning, R. (1968). *The Technique of Clear Writing* (Mc Graw-Hill).

Gupta, V. and Lehal, G. S. (2009). A survey of text mining techniques and applications, *Journal of Emerging Technologies in Web Intelligence* 1, 1, pp. 60–76.

Hahn, U. and Romacker, M. (2001). The syndikate text knowledge base generator, in *Proceedings of the first international conference on Human language technology research* (Association for Computational Linguistics), pp. 1–6.

Hassan, A. and Radev, D. (2010). Identifying text polarity using random walks, in *Proceedings of the 48th Annual Meeting of the Association for Computational Linguistics* (Association for Computational Linguistics), pp. 395–403.

Hatzivassiloglou, V. and McKeown, K. R. (1997). Predicting the semantic orientation of adjectives, in *Proceedings of the 35th Annual Meeting of the Association for Computational Linguistics and Eighth Conference of the European Chapter of the Association for Computational Linguistics* (Association for Computational Linguistics), pp. 174–181.

Hatzivassiloglou, V. and Wiebe, J. M. (2000). Effects of adjective orientation and gradability on sentence subjectivity, in *Proceedings of the 18th conference on Computational Linguistics - Volume 1* (Association for Computational Linguistics), pp. 299–305.

Hatzivassiloglou, V. and Wiebe, J. M. (2004). Towards answering opinion questions: Separating facts from opinions and identifying the polarity of opinion sentences, in *Proceedings of the 42nd annual meeting on Association for Computational Linguistics* (Association for Computational Linguistics), pp. 271–278.

Hatzivassiloglou, V. and Wiebe, J. M. (2005). Automatic detection of opinion bearing words and sentences, in *Proceedings of International Joint Conference on Natural Language Processing*, pp. 61–66.

Hu, M. and Liu, B. (2004a). Mining and summarizing customer reviews, in *Proceedings of the tenth ACM SIGKDD international conference on Knowledge discovery and data mining* (ACM), pp. 168–177.

Hu, M. and Liu, B. (2004b). Mining opinion features in customer reviews, *National Conference on Artifical Intelligence* **69**, 4735, pp. 755–760.

Jin, W. and Ho, H. H. (2009). A novel lexicalized hmm-based learning framework for web opinion mining, in *Proceedings of the 26th International Conference on Machine Learning* (International Machine Learning Society), pp. 465–472.

Jindal, N. and Liu, B. (2007). Analyzing and detecting review spam, in *Proceedings of the Seventh IEEE International Conference on Data Mining* (IEEE), pp. 547–552.

Jindal, N. and Liu, B. (2008). Opinion spam and analysis, in *Proceedings of the international conference on Web search and web data mining* (ACM), pp. 219–230.

Jindal, N., Liu, B., and Ee-Peng, L. (2010). Finding unusual review patterns using unexpected rules. in *Proceedings of the 19th ACM international conference on Information and knowledge management* (ACM), pp. 1549–1552.

Kamps, J., Marx, M., Mokken, R., and de Rijke, M. (2004). Using wordnet to measure semantic orientations of adjectives, in *Proceedings of fourth international conference on Language Resources and Evaluation*, Vol. 4 (European Language Resources Association (ELRA)), pp. 1115–1118.

Kanayama, H. and Nasukawa, T. (2006). Fully automatic lexicon expansion for domain-oriented sentiment analysis, in *Proceedings of the 2006 Conference on Empirical Methods in Natural Language Processing* (Association for Computational Linguistics), pp. 355–363.

Kempe, D., Kleinberg, J., and Tardos, É. (2003). Maximizing the spread of influence through a social network, in *Proceedings of the ninth ACM SIGKDD international conference on Knowledge discovery and data mining* (ACM), pp. 137–146.

Kim, S.-M. and Hovy, E. (2006). Identifying and analyzing judgment opinions, in *Proceedings of the main conference on Human Language Technology Conference of the North American Chapter of the Association of Computational Linguistics* (Association for Computational Linguistics), pp. 200–207.

Kim, S.-M. and Hovy, E. H. (2007). Crystal: Analyzing predictive opinions on the web, in *Proceedings of the 2007 Joint Conference on Empirical Methods in Natural Language Processing and Computational Natural Language Learning* (Association for Computational Linguistics), pp. 1056–1064.

Kim, S.-M., Pantel, P., Chklovski, T., and Pennacchiotti, M. (2006). Automatically assessing review helpfulness, in *Proceedings of the Conference on Empirical Methods in Natural Language Processing* (Association for Computational Linguistics), pp. 423–430.

Kobayashi, N., Inuui, K., and Matsumoto, Y. (2007). Extracting aspect-evaluation and aspect-of relations in opinion mining, in *Proceedings of the 2007 Joint Conference on Empirical Methods in Natural Language Processing and Computational Natural Language Learning* (Association for Computational Linguistics), pp. 1065–1074.

Krogh, A., Vedelsby, J., et al. (1995). Neural network ensembles, cross validation, and active learning, *Advances in neural information processing systems*, pp. 231–238.

Lee, K., Caverlee, J., and Webb, S. (2010). Uncovering social spammers: social honeypots + machine learning, in *Proceedings of the 33rd international ACM SIGIR conference on Research and development in information retrieval* (ACM), pp. 435–442.

Leopold, E. and Kindermann, J. (2002). Text categorization with support vector machines. How to represent texts in input space? *Machine Learning* **46**, 1–3, pp. 423–444.

Lewis, D. D. and Ringuette, M. (1994). A comparison of two learning algorithms for text categorization, in *Third annual symposium on document analysis and information retrieval*, Vol. 33, pp. 81–93.

Li, F., Han, C., Huang, M., Zhu, X., Xia, Y.-J., Zhang, S., and Yu, H. (2010a). Structure-aware review mining and summarization, in *Proceedings of the 23rd International*

Conference on Computational Linguistics (Association for Computational Linguistics), pp. 653–661.

Li, F., Huang, M., Yang, Y., and Zhu, X. (2011). Learning to identify review spam, in *Proceedings of the 22nd international joint conference on Artificial Intelligence* (AAAI Press), pp. 2488–2493.

Li, H. (2012). *Statistical Learning Methods (in Chinese)* (Tsinghua Unibersity Press).

Li, S., Huang, C.-R., Zhou, G., and Lee, S. Y. M. (2010b). Employing personal/impersonal views in supervised and semi-supervised sentiment classification, in *Proceedings of the 48th annual meeting of the association for computational linguistics* (Association for Computational Linguistics), pp. 414–423.

Li, S. and Zong, C. (2008). Multi-domain sentiment classification, in *Proceedings of the 46th Annual Meeting of the Association for Computational Linguistics on Human Language Technologies: Short Papers* (Association for Computational Linguistics), pp. 257–260.

Lim, E.-P., Nguyen, V.-A., Jindal, N., Liu, B., and Lauw, H. W. (2010). Detecting product review spammers using rating behaviors, in *Proceedings of the 19th ACM International conference on Information and knowledge management* (ACM), pp. 939–948.

Lin, D. (2003). Dependency-based evaluation of minipar, in *Volume 20 of the series Text, Speech and Language Technology* (Springer), pp. 317–329.

Lin, H. and Bilmes, J. (2011). A class of submodular functions for document summarization, in *Proceedings of the 49th Annual Meeting of the Association for Computational Linguistics*, pp. 510–520.

Lin, Y., Wang, X., Zhang, J., and Zhou, A. (2012a). Assembling the optimal sentiment classifiers, in *Web Information Systems Engineering - WISE 2012* (Springer), pp. 271–283.

Lin, Y., Zhang, J., Wang, X., and Zhou, A. (2012b). An information theoretic approach to sentiment polarity classification, in *Proceedings of the 2nd Joint WICOW/AIRWeb Workshop on Web Quality* (ACM), pp. 35–40.

Lin, Y., Zhang, J., Wang, X., and Zhou, A. (2012c). Sentiment classification via integrating multiple feature presentations, in *Proceedings of the 21st international conference companion on World Wide Web* (ACM), pp. 569–570.

Lita, L. V., Schlaikjer, A. H., Hong, W., and Nyberg, E. (2005). Qualitative dimensions in question answering: Extending the definitional qa task, in *AAAI'05 Proceedings of the 20th national conference on Artificial intelligence*, Vol. 4 (AAAI Press), pp. 1616–1617.

Liu, B., Hsu, W., and Ma, Y. (1998). Integrating classification and association rule mining, in *Proceedings of the ninth ACM SIGKDD international conference on Knowledge discovery and data mining*, pp. 80–86.

Liu, B., Hu, M., and Cheng, J. (2005). Opinion observer: analyzing and comparing opinions on the web, in *Proceedings of the 14th international conference on World Wide Web* (ACM), pp. 342–351.

Liu, J., Cao, Y., Lin, C.-Y., and Huang, Y. (2007). Low-quality product review detection in opinion summarization, in *Proceedings of the 2007 Joint Conference on Empirical Methods in Natural Language Processing and Computational Natural Language Learning*, pp. 334–342.

Liu, K., Xu, L., and Zhao, J. (2014). Extracting opinion targets and opinion words from online reviews with graph co-ranking, in *Proceedings of the 52nd Annual Meeting of the Association for Computational Linguistics* (Association for Computational Linguistics), pp. 314–324.

Liu, Y., Huang, X., An, A., and Yu, X. (2008). Modeling and predicting the helpfulness of online reviews, in *the Eighth IEEE International Conference on Data Mining* (IEEE), pp. 443–452.

Lovász, L. (1983). Submodular functions and convexity, in *Mathematical Programming The State of the Art* (Springer), pp. 235–257.

Lu, Y., Castellanos, M., Dayal, U., and Zhai, C. (2011). Automatic construction of a context-aware sentiment lexicon: an optimization approach, in *Proceedings of the 20th international conference on World Wide Web* (ACM), pp. 347–356.

Lu, Y., Tsaparas, P., Ntoulas, A., and Polanyi, L. (2010). Exploiting social context for review quality prediction, in *Proceedings of the 19th international conference on World wide web* (ACM), pp. 691–700.

Lu, Y., Zhai, C., and Sundaresan, N. (2009). Rated aspect summarization of short comments, in *Proceedings of the 18th international conference on World Wide Web* (ACM), pp. 131–140.

Martineau, J., Finin, T., Joshi, A., and Patel, S. (2009). Improving binary classification on text problems using differential word features, in *Proceedings of the 18th ACM conference on Information and knowledge management* (ACM), pp. 2019–2024.

Matsumoto, S., Takamura, H., and Okumura, M. (2005). Sentiment classification using word sub-sequences and dependency sub-trees, in *Advances in Knowledge Discovery and Data Mining* (Springer), pp. 301–311.

McLahghlin1, G. H. (1969). Smog granding: A new readability formula, *Journal of Reading* **12**, 8, pp. 639–646.

Mei, Q., Ling, X., Wondra, M., Su, H., and Zhai, C. (2007). Topic sentiment mixture: Modeling facets and opinion in weblog, in *Proceedings of the 16th international conference on World Wide Web* (ACM), pp. 171–180.

Mihalcea, R., Banea, C., and Wiebe, J. (2007). Learning multilingual subjective language via cross-lingual projections, in *ANNUAL MEETING-ASSOCIATION FOR COMPUTATIONAL LINGUISTICS*, Vol. 45, pp. 976–983.

Miller, G. A., Beckwith, R., Fellbaum, C., Gross, D., and Miller, K. J. (1990). Introduction to wordnet: An on-line lexical database, *International Journal of Lexicography* **3**, 4, pp. 235–244.

Mishne, G. and de Rijke, M. (2006). Capturing global mood levels using blog posts, in *AAAI Spring Symposium: Computational Approaches to Analyzing Weblogs*, pp. 145–152.

Mishra, A. and Rastogi, R. (2012). Semi-supervised correction of biased comment ratings, in *Proceedings of the 21st international conference on World Wide Web*, pp. 181–190.

Mudambi, S. M. and Schuff, D. (2010). What makes a helpful online review? A study of customer reviews on amazon.com, *MIS Quarterly* **34**, 1, pp. 185–200.

Mukherjee, A., Liu, B., and Glance, N. (2012). Spotting fake reviewer groups in consumer reviews, in *Proceedings of the 21st international conference on World Wide Web* (ACM), pp. 191–200.

Mukherjee, A., Liu, B., Wang, J., Glance, N., and Jindal, N. (2011). Detecting group review spam, in *Proceedings of the 20th international conference companion on World Wide Web* (ACM), pp. 93–94.

Mullen, T. and Collier, N. (2004). Sentiment analysis using support vector machines with diverse information sources. in *Proceedings of the 2004 Conference on Empirical Methods in Natural Language Processing*, Vol. 4, pp. 412–418.

Narasimhan, M. and Bilmes, J. (2007). Local search for balanced submodular clusterings. in *IJCAI*, pp. 981–986.

Nelson, P. (1970). Information and consumer behavior, *The Journal of Political Economy* **78**, 2, pp. 311–329.

Ott, M., Choi, Y., Cardie, C., and Hancock, J. T. (2011). Finding deceptive opinion spam by any stretch of the imagination, *arXiv preprint arXiv:1107.4557* .

Otterbacher, J. (2009). 'Helpfulness' in online communities: a measure of message quality, in *Proceedings of the SIGCHI Conference on Human Factor in Computing Systems* (ACM), pp. 955–964.

P O'Mahony, M. and Smyth, B. (2009). Learning to recommend helpful hotel reviews, in *Proceedings of the third ACM conference on Recommender Systems* (ACM), pp. 305–308.

Paltoglou, G. and Thelwall, M. (2010). A study of information retrieval weighting schemes for sentiment analysis, in *Proceedings of the 48th Annual Meeting of the Association for Computational Linguistics* (Association for Computational Linguistics), pp. 1386–1395.

Pan, S. J., Ni, X., Sun, J.-T., Yang, Q., and Chen, Z. (2010). Cross-domain sentiment classification via spectral feature alignment, in *Proceedings of the 19th international conference on World Wide Web* (ACM), pp. 751–760.

Pang, B. and Lee, L. (2004). A sentimental education: Sentiment analysis using subjectivity summarization based on minimum cuts, in *Proceedings of the 42nd annual meeting on Association for Computational Linguistics* (Association for Computational Linguistics), pp. 271–278.

Pang, B. and Lee, L. (2008). Opinion mining and sentiment analysis, *Foundations and trends in information retrieval* **2**, 1–2, pp. 1–135.

Pang, B., Lee, L., and Vaithyanathan, S. (2002). Thumbs up?: Sentiment classification using machine learning techniques, in *Proceedings of the ACL-02 conference on Empirical methods in natural language processing - Volume 10* (Association for Computational Linguistics), pp. 79–86.

Popescu, A.-M. and Etzioni, O. (2007). Extracting product features and opinions from reviews, in *Natural language processing and text mining* (Springer), pp. 9–28.

Poria, S., Cambria, E., Ku, L., and Gui, A., Chen, G. and Gelbukh, A. (2014). A rule-based approach to aspect extraction from product reviews, in *Proceedings of the Second Workshop on Natural Language Processing for Social Media (SocialNLP)*, pp. 28–37.

Qiu, G., Liu, B., Bu, J., and Chen, C. (2011). Opinion word expansion and target extraction through double propagation, *Computational Linguistics* **37**, 1, pp. 9–27.

Quinlan, J. R. (1986). Induction of decision trees, *Machine Learning* **1**, 1, pp. 81–106.

Quinlan, J. R. (1993). *C4. 5: programs for machine learning*, Vol. 1 (Morgan kaufmann).

Ravi, S. S., Rosenkrantz, D. J., and Tayi, G. K. (1994). Heuristic and special case algorithms for dispersion problems, *Operations Research* **42**, 2, pp. 299–310.

Schütze, H., Hull, D. A., and Pedersen, J. O. (1995). A comparison of classifiers and document representations for the routing problem, in *Proceedings of the 18th annual international ACM SIGIR conference on Research and development in information retrieval* (ACM), pp. 229–237.

Siersdorfer, S., Chelaru, S., Nejdl, W., and Pedro, J. S. (2010). How useful are your comments?: Analyzing and predicting youtube comments and comment ratings, in *Proceedings of the 19th international conference on World Wide Web* (ACM), pp. 891–900.

Skalak, D. B. (1996). The sources of increased accuracy for two proposed boosting algorithms, in *Proceedings of the American Association for Artificial Intelligence, AAAI-96, Integrating Multiple Learned Models Workshop*, Vol. 1129 (Citeseer), p. 1133.

Smith, E. and Senter, R. (1962). Automated readability index, *Aerospace Medical Research Laboratories*, pp. 1–14.

Somasundaran, S., Wilson, T., Wiebe, J., and Stoyanov, V. (2007). QA with attitude: Exploiting opinion type analysis for improving question answering in on-line discussions and the news. In Intl Conference on weblogs & Social, in *Proceedings of the international conference on Web search and web data mining*. Boulder, Colorado, USA, March 26–28, 2007.

Stoyanov, V. and Cardie, C. (2008). Topic identification for fine-grained opinion analysis, in *Proceedings of the 22nd International Conference on Computational Linguistics* (Association for Computational Linguistics), pp. 817–824.

Stoyanov, V., Cardie, C., and Wiebe, J. (2005). Multi-perspective question answering using the opqa corpus, in *Proceedings of the conference on Human Language Technology and Empirical Methods in Natural Language Processing* (Association for Computational Linguistics), pp. 923–930.

Su, F. and Markert, K. (2009). Subjectivity recognition on word senses via semi-supervised mincuts, in *Proceedings of Human Language Technologies: The 2009 Annual Conference of the North American Chapter of the Association for Computational Linguistics* (Association for Computational Linguistics), pp. 1–9.

Takamura, H., Inui, T., and Okumura, M. (2006). Latent variable models for semantic orientations of phrases, in *Conference on European Chapter of the Association for Computational Linguistics* (Association for Computational Linguistics), pp. 201–208.

Tan, C., Lee, L., Tang, J., Jiang, L., Zhou, M., and Li, P. (2011). User-level sentiment analysis incorporating social networks, in *Proceedings of the 17th ACM SIGKDD international conference on Knowledge discovery and data mining* (ACM), pp. 1397–1405.

Tan, S. and Cheng, X. (2009). Improving SCL model for sentiment-transfer learning, in *Proceedings of Human Language Technologies: The 2009 Annual Conference of the North American Chapter of the Association for Computational Linguistics, Companion Volume: Short Papers* (Association for Computational Linguistics), pp. 181–184.

Tang, H., Tan, S., and Cheng, X. (2009). A survey on sentiment detection of reviews, *Expert Systems with Applications* **36**, 7, pp. 10760–10773.

Tang, J., Gao, H., Hu, X., and Liu, H. (2013). Context-aware review helpfulness rating prediction, in *Proceedings of the 7th ACM Conference on Recommender Systems* (ACM), pp. 1–8.

Titov, I. and McDonald, R. (2008). A joint model of text and aspect ratings for sentiment summarization, in *Proceedings of ACL-08:HLT* (Association for Computational Linguistics), pp. 308–316.

Tsur, O. and Rappoport, A. (2009). Revrank: A fully unsupervised algorithm for selecting the most helpful book reviews, in *Proceedings of the 3rd AAAI Conference on Weblogs and Social Media*, pp. 154–161.

Turney, P. D. (2002). Thumbs up or thumbs down?: semantic orientation applied to unsupervised classification of reviews, in *Proceedings of the 40th annual meeting on association for computational linguistics* (Association for Computational Linguistics), pp. 417–424.

Vee, E., Srivastava, U., Shanmugasundaram, J., Bhat, P., and Yahia, S. A. (2008). Efficient computation of diverse query results, in *Proceedings of the 24th International Conference on Data Engineering* (IEEE), pp. 228–236.

Venkatasubramanian, S., Veilumuthu, A., Krishnamurthy, A., Madhavan, C. E. V., Nath, K., and Arvindam, S. (2011). A non-syntactic approach for text sentiment classification with stopwords, in *Proceedings of the 20th international conference companion on World Wide Web* (ACM), pp. 137–138.

Wang, B. and Wang, H. (2008). Bootstrapping both product features and opinion words from chinese customer reviews with cross-inducing, in *The 7th Internatioanl Joint Conference on Natural Language Processing of the Asian Federation of Natural Language Processing* (Association for Computational Linguistics), pp. 289–295.

Wang, G., Xie, S., Liu, B., and Yu, P. S. (2012). Identify online store review spammers via social review graph, *ACM Transactions on Intelligent Systems and Technology (TIST)* 3, 4, p. 61.

Wei, W. and Gulla, J. A. (2010). Sentiment learning on product reviews via sentiment ontology tree, in *Proceedings of the 48th Annual Meeting of the Association for Computational Linguistics* (Association for Computational Linguistics), pp. 404–413.

Weimer, M., Gurevych, I., and Mühlhäuser, M. (2007). Automatically assessing the post quality in online discussions on software, in *Proceedings of the 45th Annual Meeting of the ACL on Interactive Poster and Demonstration Sessions* (Association for Computational Linguistics), pp. 125–128.

Wiener, E., Pedersen, J. O., Weigend, A. S., et al. (1995). A neural network approach to topic spotting, in *Proceedings of the 4th annual symposium on document analysis and information retrieval*, pp. 317–332.

Wilson, T., Hoffmann, P., Somasundaran, S., Kessler, J., Wiebe, J., Choi, Y., Cardie, C., Riloff, E., and Patwardhan, S. (2005). Opinionfinder: A system for subjectivity analysis, in *Proceedings of HLT/EMNLP 2005 Demonstration Abstracts* (Association for Computational Linguistics), pp. 34–35.

Wu, G., Greene, D., and Cunningham, P. (2010a). Merging multiple criteria to identify suspicious reviews, in *Proceedings of the fourth ACM conference on Recommender systems* (ACM), pp. 241–244.

Wu, G., Greene, D., Smyth, B., and Cunningham, P. (2010b). Distortion as a validation criterion in the identification of suspicious reviews, in *Proceedings of the First Workshop on Social Media Analytics* (ACM), pp. 10–13.

Wu, Q., Tan, S., Cheng, X., and Duan, M. (2010c). Miea: a mutual iterative enhancement approach for cross-domain sentiment classification, in *Proceedings of the 23rd International Conference on Computational Linguistics: Posters* (Association for Computational Linguistics), pp. 1327–1335.

Xia, R., Zong, C., and Li, S. (2011). Ensemble of feature sets and classification algorithms for sentiment classification, *Information Sciences* **181**, 6, pp. 1138–1152.

Xie, S., Wang, G., Lin, S., and Yu, P. S. (2012). Review spam detection via temporal pattern discovery, in *Proceedings of the 18th ACM SIGKDD international conference on Knowledge discovery and data mining* (ACM), pp. 823–831.

Xu, L., Li, B., and Chen, E. (2012). Ensemble pruning via constrained eigen-optimization, in *Proceedings of the 12th International Conference on Data Mining* (IEEE), pp. 715–724.

Yang, Y. (1995). Noise reduction in a statistical approach to text categorization, in *Proceedings of the 18th annual international ACM SIGIR conference on Research and development in information retrieval* (ACM), pp. 256–263.

Yang, Y. and Pedersen, J. O. (1997). A comparative study on feature selection in text categorization, in *Proceedings of the 14th International Conference on Machine Learning* (International Machine Learning Society), pp. 412–420.

Yao, T., Nie, Q., Li, J., Li, L., Lou, D., Chen, K., and Fu, Y. (2006). An opinion mining system for chinese automobile reviews (in chinese), *Frontiers of Chinese Information Processing*, pp. 260–281.

Yi, J., Nasukawa, T., Bunescu, R., and Niblack, W. (2003). Sentiment analyzer: Extracting sentiments about a given topic using natural language processing techniques, in *Third IEEE International Conference on Data Mining*, (IEEE), pp. 427–434.

Yi, J. and Niblack, W. (2005). Sentiment mining in webfountain, in *Proceedings of the 21st International Conference on Data Engineering* (IEEE), pp. 1073–1083.

Zenko, B., Todorovski, L., and Dzeroski, S. (2001). A comparison of stacking with meta decision trees to bagging, boosting, and stacking with other methods, in *Proceedings IEEE International Conference on Data Mining, 2001.* (IEEE), pp. 669–670.

Zhang, Z. and Varadarajan, B. (2006). Utility scoring of product reviews, in *Proceedings of the 15th ACM international conference on Information and knowledge management* (ACM), pp. 51–57.

Zhuang, L., Jing, F., and Zhu, X. (2006). Movie review mining and summarization, in *Proceedings of the 15th ACM international conference on Information and knowledge management* (ACM), pp. 43–50.

Index

Printed in the United States
By Bookmasters